WORK HAPPY
LIVE HEALTHY

Losing my job after sixteen years was a very traumatic experience. You helped me tremendously in assessing my skills, abilities, and accomplishments. I attribute the successful outcome of my job search to you and your strategies. You helped me realize how much I had to offer.

Rosalie Pratesi, Administrative Assistant

I was so excited at how quickly things happened after I read *Work Happy Live Healthy*, that I couldn't sleep. You helped me find the job of my dreams, and I doubled my salary.

Jonathan Zide, Marketing Consultant

In a very structured way, your book helped me answer one of the most difficult questions I faced: "What to do for the rest of my life?"

Ed Binkerd, Vice President of Human Resources

Thank you for your contribution to my current successes. I went from career depression to finding my perfect niche. I sincerely believe I would not have sought this path without your *Work Happy Live Healthy* solutions.

Ken Lehman, Physical Therapist

I had not interviewed for a job in five years. You helped me take control of the process right from the beginning and you explained things in a manner which encouraged me to take steps I was reluctant to take. *Work Happy Live Healthy* is exceptional.

Sandra Faust, Ph.D., Director Clinical Operations Behavioral Health

You made it abundantly clear that life is too short to not enjoy your job. And you made it fun to change. I've just found a new job I love... if I can do it, anyone can!

Mark Lombardi, Pharmacy Director

WORK HAPPY LIVE HEALTHY

NEW SOLUTIONS FOR CAREER SATISFACTION

INCLUDING *MORE TIME & MONEY*

TOM WELCH

Rhodes & Easton

Traverse City, Michigan

Published by RHODES & EASTON
121 E. Front Street, 4th Floor, Traverse City, Michigan 49684

Publisher's Cataloging-in-Publication Data
Welch, Tom.
    Work happy live healthy: new solutions for career satisfaction, including more time and money / Tom Welch ; foreword by Sue Shellenbarger. --
Traverse City, MI : Rhodes & Easton, 1997.
        p.   cm.
    Includes bibliographical references and index.
    ISBN 0-9649401-6-7
    1. Job hunting. 2. Career Development.   3. Success in business. I. Title.
HF5382.7.W45 1997
650.14 dc—20   96-71010

Editorial development by Mary Jo Buday
PROJECT COORDINATION BY JENKINS GROUP

99 98 97 ❖ 5 4 3 2 1

Printed in the United States of America

Dedicated to you and your desire for personal fulfillment, a sense of well-being, health, and abundance in all areas of your life.

Contents

Foreword

Few things are more important to Americans' sense of identity and personal worth than work. We are a nation of workers. We seek purpose, meaning, and self-esteem in our work. Hard workers are our cultural heroes.

Yet in my own work as a specialist in workplace issues, both as a national newspaper columnist and syndicated radio talk-show host, I regularly encounter people who are profoundly demoralized about the way they make a living. Buffeted by global economic forces beyond their control—downward pressure on pay and prices, unrelenting lay offs, employer demands for longer hours and higher output—many workers have lost sight of the intrinsic personal value of work. Stress and burnout, and the health problems they cause, are mounting. Workplace morale at many employers has hit the skids. To many, experiencing the real joy of work, not just as a means to a paycheck but as an expression of oneself in society, seems an elusive goal.

This book promises to help readers find their own personal path toward that goal. Tom Welch distills the wisdom of many years' professional experience to offer a kind of "essential career coach" between two covers—a guide to self-discovery that you can carry with you, read in crisis or at leisure, and consult again and again at new stages of life. Like a warm talk with a wise and insightful friend, the pages that follow will hearten and guide you on a step-by-step uncovering of the unique skills and talents you most enjoy using, the career values you hold dear, and the attitudes and strategies you need to manifest them in your life. As challenging as it may be, following the path to self-discovery Tom maps out is essential to defining and experiencing the joy of work—and for many of us, the joy of life.

Anyone who has worked for long will recognize himself or herself in this book. Tom has spent years in the career trenches, counseling people at the most discouraging and most exhilarating stages of their work lives, and he recounts the most illuminating of those stories: the bored dentist who discovered a second profession, the defeated layoff victim who learned to savor his newly-acquired professional skills, the directionless human resource manager who found new purpose in transferring to a different function, and the pink-slipped factory workers who found ways to get past their anger and move on.

Those who are fortunate enough to do work they love will recognize and appreciate the truth here. Those who aren't will learn how to seek it—to undertake the challenge of discovering your life's work in its essence, as author Joseph Conrad defined it nearly a century ago, as "the chance to find yourself. Your own reality—for yourself, not for others—what no other man can ever know."

Sue Shellenbarger
National Newspaper Columnist
& Syndicated Talk Show Host

Introduction

Why do some people seem so happy? Why do they enjoy their jobs so much that their work seems like play? How does *your* job make you feel? Do you love your job? Are you proud of what you do? Are you having fun in your profession? Are you paid what you are worth? Do you look forward to the start of each work day?

Is your job *just* a job—and not a *passion*? If so, you're probably in the wrong profession. Most of us begin our careers by chance. We aren't necessarily well-suited for our professions in the first place!

The pursuit of unsuitable careers makes many peoples' lives miserable. Have you ever not wanted to get out of bed, because you didn't want to go to work? There is no greater waste of time and energy than going to an eight or ten or twelve-hour-a-day job that makes you feel bad. If you don't like your job, I guarantee these negative feelings affect every aspect of your life, including your: self-esteem, business and personal relationships, health, and earning power.

Work Anxiety

Approximately eight-five percent of the work force is disenchanted with their job or career. In a recent *U.S. News & World Report* survey, people were asked how happy they were with their lives. People were overwhelmingly dissatisfied with their jobs, finances, and leisure time.

11

The *source* of most people's dissatisfaction *is* their job. Finances are intrinsically linked with a job, and discontentment with your job influences your leisure time. Do you feel underpaid and overworked? How often do you find yourself dwelling about a work issue when you're supposed to be relaxing?

Problems with work, money, and leisure time are evident in all class levels. Too many people are doing what they don't like to do, with little or no sense of accomplishment, and for less money than they are worth. The result is a tremendous amount of anxiety throughout the work force.

You are probably experiencing at least some of these feelings yourself. Maybe you've been downsized, re-engineered, or fired. Maybe you're underpaid, overworked, under-utilized, or bored. No matter the cause of your frustration, you truly *want* to make changes in your life, but you don't know what to do.

Negative work emotions will carry over into the rest of your life. Your self-esteem will suffer. Your relationships (both business and personal) will be impacted. Studies even show that your children's behavior is influenced by your job happiness! When parents don't enjoy their jobs, their children are less stable emotionally and exhibit more behavioral problems.

Outwardly, you might appear successful, but you don't like who you are or what you've become.

Solution

What's the solution? It begins with the realization that there *is* a career or a job out there that represents your path in life. There *is* a job which will give you a sense of purpose, increased earnings, and a renewed sense of balance—at home and at work. Working in the right job will produce enormous satisfaction, which will be reflected in all areas of your life. You will experience personal growth and freedom, more control, a renewed sense of success, and more energy for relationships.

Why don't more people have jobs like this? It's not for a lack of talent or skills or ambition. What most people lack is a sense of *direction*. They need a guide to assist them on their journey...someone or something to help them achieve the changes they would like to make in their life. They need a clear, simple, and effective plan of *action* to move toward greater fulfillment, happiness, health, and prosperity.

I've been providing professional career and life guidance to people since the early 1970s, when I began to notice that, in general, people were under a great amount of job-related stress. Many people had lost their jobs; others were so dissatisfied with their choice of careers, that their entire lives where negatively affected. Worst of all, they seemed resigned to their unhappiness. They had no direction—no mission—and no one to turn to for help.

I observed these people. I studied how they viewed life, what role their jobs played in their lives, how their emotions and beliefs affected their thinking, how they perceived change, and how they entered into their careers in the first place. After many years of research, I developed solutions; simple and easy-to-follow strategies to help people get from where they are today to where they want to be tomorrow.

Faster, Easier, Better

Choosing the right career and finding the best job offer doesn't have to be complicated. You don't have to spend weeks or months reading large volumes of resource material, trying to figure out how to find a job that is well-suited to your talents. This book will instruct you on how to use specific self-promotion strategies, so you can maximize the results of your efforts. There's also an added bonus: the simple process you'll learn is fun to do!

Thousands of people have used the principles in this book to achieve what they wanted—and they are now living much happier and fulfilling lives. They have turned their work into play.

You have the opportunity to change your disenchantment to excitement. You don't want to reach retirement age and say to yourself, "Is that all there is? I could have done so much more with my life."

Work Happy...Live Healthy

Job happiness and life fulfillment are possible. I'll show you how to obtain them. There are specific actions you can take which will lead you to greater satisfaction, enhanced job security, increased earnings, more control of your life, improved relationships, better health, more fun, more leisure time, and less stress and frustration. But before you take these actions (to get from where you are today to where you want to be tomorrow), you first need to determine if your job and career are right for you.

What You'll Learn

That's what this book is all about: discovering who you really are, identifying what you want out of your job and your life, and learning how to achieve it. I will take the whole process of determining what it is you're meant to do in life, and break it into pieces so it's easy to understand and simple for you to do. You'll learn how to discover your values— what is important for you to be happy in a job. You will learn the critical role your values play in job selection and job satisfaction.

You will learn how your beliefs control your emotions *and* your thinking. You will learn how to change your thinking, and thus, control your feelings about anything in life—which can dramatically increase your happiness and energy level.

You will learn techniques to eliminate fear. No longer will the fear of rejection prevent you from acting on your desires. You'll be able to use the techniques immediately and you will experience instantaneous results.

I guarantee there is nothing that will bring you more joy, more excitement, and more success than knowing what you are meant to do—and then doing it! Taking action is the number one key to success.

After spending many years advising companies on their hiring practices, combined with my expertise in Retained Executive Search, I know what does and doesn't work in the job search process. I will share proven strategies to help you accelerate and maximize your job search efforts. In the process, I'll guide you through the nineteen deadly sins of job searching.

You will learn personal marketing techniques which will lift you miles above the crowd, including designing a top-notch resume. I'll show you how to have a job created for you, even if one doesn't exist. You will learn how to present yourself in an interview, so that you get the offer you want. You'll learn how to negotiate the best possible salary and benefit package; and how to evaluate the job offer, to assure it is a job you want.

Once you understand the ease of these strategies—and the potential benefit to you—nothing will stop you from creating your future. It doesn't matter if you are an executive, a technician, an assembly line worker, a carpenter, a law enforcement officer, a salesperson, or a teacher—you can easily make these formulas work for you. Maybe you will decide to change jobs or careers. Maybe you will modify your present position; or maybe you will decide that owning your own business is what's best.

As you embark on your journey, remember I am here to help you. Contact me anytime with questions or concerns. And, don't forget to tell me about your victories. I love a good success story.

You *can* love your work, gain control over your future, earn more money, and live a happier, healthier life. All it takes is a little planning and some focused action. Get excited! Get from where you are today to where you want to be tomorrow.

Tom Welch

Career Dimensions, Inc.
900 E. Ocean Blvd., #232
Stuart, FL 34994
(561) 288-1811

Part One

Evaluating Your Talents

Throughout this book you will be guided through several exercises which require thinking and writing on your part. Although "workbook" pages are provided after each exercise, I strongly suggest you purchase a Work Happy Live Healthy Workbook *(see page 255) or a spiral notebook. The dimensions of this book shouldn't place a limit on your ideas or the length of your notes.*

Discovering Your Skills And Talents

Have you ever taken the time to figure out who you really are and what you can truly do? To enjoy happiness and success it is critical that *you* know yourself well. You're probably thinking, "What does he mean? I've known *me* since I was born. I know what I can and can't do."

Are you sure?

I worked with a young man whose administrative position at a major corporation was being phased out. Like so many other people, he had never identified or evaluated his skills. As a result, he was very apprehensive about looking for a new job. However, once I helped him discover his talents and skills, his job search became easier and much more effective. He quickly found an opportunity with a new company.

By chance, I met this gentleman a few months later. The first thing he said to me was, "I'm feeling great. I used to be so stressed by the possibility of being laid off from my last company, that my whole life was affected. I hated going to work. Now that I know my skills and have confidence in my abilities, I don't worry about being laid off anymore.

"I really like my new job, it's interesting and fun. But if something happened and they laid me off tomorrow, I know I can go out and contribute elsewhere. I no longer fear the future."

What a great achievement he had made. By understanding his worth, he had created his own job stability. Notice, his stability came from *within himself*—it did not come from a job or a company.

Past generations could depend on their employers to provide job security. If employees performed their jobs moderately well, they could anticipate working for the same company as long as they wanted. Times have changed. Today, job security is dependent on you knowing your skills. You must have confidence in who you are and in what you can do.

Think about the thousands of high school and college students approaching graduation who don't know what they are going to do with their lives. Consider the thirty year old engineer I recently coached, who was tired of engineering but had no idea what else he could do. He didn't know if he had any other skills. What about the accountant who sat in my office after being laid off? He never felt accounting was right for him, but that's all he had ever done; he said he didn't have any other talents. Or what about the factory worker who was certain there was nothing she could do, except work on an assembly line?

Did any of these people truly understand themselves? No! In a recent survey, hiring managers stated that seventy-five percent of the job candidates they interviewed were unable to identify their skills and were unable to discuss how an employer would benefit by hiring them.

Does this sound familiar? Have you found yourself in a similar situation? An inability to identify your skills and to talk about your strengths is not solely your fault. When you were growing up, your parents probably told you not to brag about yourself. So, you didn't (and don't). And, your education probably didn't help much either. Few, if any, courses are structured to help you identify your talents.

Also, think about your transition from school to work. Did you choose your profession based on your skills and what you enjoy doing—or did the job just sort of happen? Is your job simply something that came along or is it something someone else wanted you to do?

Few people choose their jobs based on their talents, which is one reason why so many workers are dissatisfied with their work. People don't take the time to think about their talents and skills, what value they might provide to an employer, and what satisfaction they might obtain if they used their unique abilities.

A few months ago, a friend of mine asked me to meet with his daughter, Jennifer, who had recently graduated from college with a degree in communications and television production. He had arranged for his daughter to meet with an executive of a large, independent TV station. (It was strictly a courtesy interview, there weren't any job openings at the station, especially for a recent graduate.)

My friend felt that Jennifer was poorly prepared for the interview, so he asked me to give her some guidance. At the beginning of my meeting with Jennifer, I wanted to learn what her skills and talents were. "Jenn," I asked, "what are you good at?"

She thought and thought, and then finally responded, "How many things do I need to think of?"

Jennifer could not come up with *one* skill or talent! She was twenty-one years old, had accomplished quite a bit in her life, and yet was unable to easily identify her skills and talents.

To help her avoid this dilemma during her interview at the TV station, I asked Jennifer to tell me about some of the things she had done, the activities she had participated in at college, and the various clubs she had belonged to while in school. By the time we ended our discussion, we had listed *twelve* strong talents and abilities Jennifer possessed!

I then advised Jennifer on how she could communicate the worth of these talents during her interview, thereby demonstrating to the TV executive how, as an employee, she would benefit the television station. Realize, without this newly-discovered information, her interview would have been nothing more than it was set up to be: a favor, with no prospect of a job offer. However, with Jennifer's enthusiasm, heightened by the knowledge of her talents, she converted this courtesy interview into an actual job offer!

Jennifer's situation is just one example of the importance of knowing your skills and talents. (I'll give many others throughout this book.) Remember, although Jennifer's talents existed prior to her meeting with me, until I gave her the *tools of self discovery*, she was unable to identify them.

Before you begin your journey to self discovery, let's define our terms: **Talents** are innate; you were born with them. They are the abilities you have which seem to come to you naturally. For instance, your talent might be in music, sports, art, or mathematics.

Skills are abilities that have been developed or acquired through education or training. Skills can be broken down between technical skills (associated with your job) and personal skills (learned outside of your job). Some examples of job-related skills would be: operating machinery, managing people, and public speaking. Personal skills would include: gardening, shopping, budgeting, raising children, and cooking.

Traits are distinguishing qualities which are a part of your personality: dependability, honesty, patience, determination, friendliness, etc.

When you combine your talents, skills, and traits you will begin to understand your uniqueness.

For instance, you might have musical talent (which you were born with), the skill of playing the trombone (acquired from lessons and practice), and the determination (personality trait) to play better.

Now that you understand the terms, it's time to discover who you are.

Seven Steps To Self Discovery

The following seven-step self discovery formula has been used by thousands of people who were looking for greater satisfaction in their work and personal lives. If you make the commitment to devote the time and thought required to answer these questions, I guarantee it will work for you. The results will be eye-opening and they will give you the incentive to take the necessary actions to get where you want to be in life. Get your pencils and notebook ready—and have fun.

Step One
Identifying Work Accomplishments

The first step in identifying your skills and talents is to make a list of your work accomplishments. By accomplishments, I mean anything you did in a job which made you feel good. Even if you've done it over and over again since, if you felt proud the first time you did it, list it, because it *was* an accomplishment.

Some things, which you do routinely and don't consider to be a big deal (like working on a computer), are accomplishments. Many people don't have the skill, and at some point you took the initiative to learn it.

Be thorough when making your list. Don't minimize the task because it came easily to you. Ask yourself, "Would this be considered an accomplishment if someone else did it?" If your answer is "yes," include it on your list. Here are other questions to consider while you identify your work accomplishments:

❑ Have you ever won an award?

❑ Have you ever made helpful suggestions?

❑ Did you solve a problem or improve quality?

❑ Did you ever organize an event or coordinate a project?

❑ Did you help a company grow by increasing sales or reducing expenses?

❑ Did you ever simplify something or come up with a new way of doing it?

Furthermore, accomplishments don't have to be major events. They can be something simple, like: "My supervisor once told me I was the most enthusiastic person in the department."

At the top of the first page in your spiral notebook write, "Work Accomplishments." List your work accomplishments below the heading (or you may use pages 26-27). The longer you can make your list, the better. Start at the beginning of your career and include any time you might have spent in the military. List everything you can think of—and be specific.

If you're just graduating, list your accomplishments from the years you spent in school. Did you overcome a particularly difficult course or professor? Did you contribute, in some way, at a part-time job? What about other activities, like sports, fraternities, sororities, and clubs? Try to remember anything you did which made you feel proud, and include it on your list.

❧ Step Two ❧
Identifying Personal Accomplishments

The second step is to compile a list of your personal accomplishments. This list should include anything you achieved in your personal life that made you feel good. Maybe you completed a certain level of education, or you saved enough money to purchase a car or a house, or you raised your children well, or you're proud of your community involvement. Whatever it is, include it on the list.

At one of my seminars a gentleman said, "I'm not a contractor but when we built our house I coordinated the subcontractors and ordered the building materials. I ran the whole project. Would this be something to list under my personal accomplishments?"

"By all means," I said. "You used so many talents and skills to achieve your goal, it definitely belongs on your list."

Remember, though, your accomplishments do not have to be as big as this example. Something as simple as planting a garden or taking a photograph you were proud of should be listed. Take some quality time to think through what you have done. If you felt a sense of achievement, include it on your list.

At the top of the next blank, right-hand page in your spiral notebook write, "Personal Accomplishments." Compile your list below the heading, using as many pages as necessary (or use pages 28-29).

↙ Step Three ↘
Talents And Skills

After you've identified your work and personal accomplishments, you will need to determine the talents and skills you used to perform each accomplishment. For example, let's say the first work accomplishment

> "Success is not the key to happiness. Happiness is the key to success. If you love what you are doing, you will be successful."
> —Herman Cain

WORK ACCOMPLISHMENTS

1. _____
   _____
   _____

2. _____
   _____
   _____

3. _____
   _____
   _____

4. _____
   _____
   _____

5. _____
   _____
   _____

6. _____
   _____
   _____

7. _____
   _____
   _____

WORK ACCOMPLISHMENTS

8. _____

_____

_____

9. _____

_____

_____

10. _____

_____

_____

11. _____

_____

_____

12. _____

_____

_____

13. _____

_____

_____

14. _____

_____

_____

PERSONAL ACCOMPLISHMENTS

1. _____

_____

_____

2. _____

_____

_____

3. _____

_____

_____

4. _____

_____

_____

5. _____

_____

_____

6. _____

_____

_____

7. _____

_____

_____

PERSONAL ACCOMPLISHMENTS

8. _____

_____

_____

9. _____

_____

_____

10. _____

_____

_____

11. _____

_____

_____

12. _____

_____

_____

13. _____

_____

_____

14. _____

_____

_____

on your list in Step One is that you developed a new process to reduce manufacturing costs for a product by twenty percent. In Step Three you must specify the talents and skills you used to accomplish this. For underneath "Talents and Skills Used In Work Accomplishments" you would list all of these skills.

Using this same analytical process, identify the skills and talents you used to complete each of your work and personal accomplishments. List as many skills as possible for each accomplishment. If you can break a general skill into specific abilities, all the better. For example, instead of just saying "used people skills," specify what you did. Did you teach, manage, coach, assist, persuade, listen to, motivate, or communicate with people? If you communicated with people, was it spoken or written? To individuals or to groups?

If you find it difficult to identify your skills and talents, don't be discouraged. This is probably the first time in your life that you've tried to use this type of discovery process. Stay with it. You'll figure it out.

Because you were directly involved with the task, it might be difficult for you to give yourself credit for the talents you used. Therefore, try approaching the exercise from a slightly different viewpoint. Determine the skills someone else would have used to accomplish the same thing. In other words, if you had to hire someone to do the task, what talents would you look for in that person? If this approach doesn't help, and you're still unable to identify your skills, discuss your work and personal accomplishments with a relative or friend. Ask them what skills they think you used for each accomplishment.

This process requires thought and time on your part. Do not feel rushed. Take your time. The answers will come to you.

You can use pages 32-33 or on the next blank, right-hand page in your notebook write, "Talents and Skills Used in Work Accomplishments." After you have finished that list, on the next blank, right-hand page in your notebook write, "Talents and Skills Used in Personal Accomplishments," or use pages 34-35. (Each accomplishment listed in Steps One and Two should have a corresponding list of skills in Step Three.)

After you've finished both lists, you might notice that several skills and talents are repeated over and over again. For instance, verbal communication and organization might be skills you used in most of your accomplishments, while coordination and listening skills show up almost as often.

The five, six, or seven skills which have been repeated most often are probably some of the strongest skills you possess. Go ahead and circle them.

These skills are your strengths and you probably enjoy using them. They are the skills you used most often to achieve something; and people usually succeed at something because they enjoy doing it.

By working in a job that utilizes and encourages the use of these skills, you will experience more happiness and success, while enjoying a better quality of life.

Many people spend far too much time trying to correct their weaknesses, while ignoring the strengths they possess. If something comes easily to you, it's most likely one of your natural talents. Try to use it as often as you can.

⊰ Step Four ⊱
Family and Friends

Step Four in the self discovery formula is to make sure you have accurately identified your strengths. To do this, you must talk with several people who know you well—either relatives, friends, coworkers, or fellow students. Ask these individuals what *they* think your talents are. In their opinion, what are your strengths? Oftentimes friends and relatives will identify abilities and traits you don't see in yourself.

TALENTS & SKILLS USED IN WORK ACCOMPLISHMENTS

1. _____

_____

_____

2. _____

_____

_____

3. _____

_____

_____

4. _____

_____

_____

5. _____

_____

_____

6. _____

_____

_____

7. _____

_____

_____

TALENTS & SKILLS USED IN WORK ACCOMPLISHMENTS

8. _____

_____

_____

9. _____

_____

_____

10. _____

_____

_____

11. _____

_____

_____

12. _____

_____

_____

13. _____

_____

_____

14. _____

_____

_____

TALENTS & SKILLS USED IN PERSONAL ACCOMPLISHMENTS

1. _____

   _____

   _____

2. _____

   _____

   _____

3. _____

   _____

   _____

4. _____

   _____

   _____

5. _____

   _____

   _____

6. _____

   _____

   _____

7. _____

   _____

   _____

TALENTS & SKILLS USED IN
PERSONAL ACCOMPLISHMENTS

8. _____

_____

_____

9. _____

_____

_____

10. _____

_____

_____

11. _____

_____

_____

12. _____

_____

_____

13. _____

_____

_____

14. _____

_____

_____

You may be surprised at how candid these people will be. As a matter of fact, most people will enjoy helping you. (Your request for assistance might stimulate *their* curiosity, and they'll decide to identify their skills, too!)

Be sure to write down *every* opinion that is shared with you. When you have finished interviewing all of your relatives and friends, compare their comments with the talents and skills you identified in Step Three.

At the top of the next blank, right-hand page in your notebook write, "Strengths Suggested by Others," or use pages 37-38 for your notes.

↳ Step Five ↲
Past Jobs

Next you need to reflect upon your career and identify specific aspects you enjoyed about each job you held. Realize, even if you were basically unhappy with a job, there was probably something you liked about it.

For example, I once spoke with a sales manager who spent most of his time in his office dealing with administrative matters. Overall, he was very disenchanted with his job; however, he felt great satisfaction whenever he had to assist a customer. That was one part of his job which he found very enjoyable.

Take the time to think about what you liked in your jobs. Write your responses on the next blank, right-hand page in your notebook under the title, "What I Liked About Past Jobs" or use pages 40-41. (If you are a recent high school or college graduate, write down the courses and school activities you liked. Also, list what you liked about any part-time jobs you had.)

After you've completed this exercise, you need to determine the talents and skills you used in each activity. Follow the same guidelines provided in Step Three (page 30). Remember—be specific. On the next blank, right-hand page in your notebook write the title, "Talents And Skills Used Doing What I Liked" or use the pages 42-43.

STRENGTHS SUGGESTED BY OTHERS

1. _____

2. _____

3. _____

4. _____

5. _____

6. _____

7. _____

8. _____

9. _____

10. _____

11. _____

12. _____

13. _____

14. _____

15. _____

16. _____

17. _____

18. _____

STRENGTHS SUGGESTED BY OTHERS

19. _____

20. _____

21. _____

22. _____

23. _____

24. _____

25. _____

26. _____

27. _____

28. _____

29. _____

30. _____

31. _____

32. _____

33. _____

34. _____

35. _____

36. _____

↫ Step Six ↬
Leisure Time

Now it's time to identify the leisure time activities which bring you pleasure. In your notebook, title the next blank, right-hand page, "Leisure Time Activities I Enjoy." (Or use pages 44-45.) List the activities you like to do on your time off. Keep in mind: what motivates you in your leisure hours can provide great clues to your talents and interests.

Once you've completed your list of pleasurable leisure time activities, you'll need to determine the talents and skills you use for each activity.

For example, I recently consulted with a gentleman who worked as an accountant. During his leisure time, he found great relaxation while cooking. He liked the creativity he used in the kitchen and he enjoyed the detail that went into preparing a gourmet dish. He liked the fact that he was responsible for the results; and, he found complete satisfaction in serving a meal which pleased his guests—and one on which they highly complimented him. (This one leisure time activity reveals much about his talents, skills, and traits.)

Be thorough when identifying the skills and talents you use in your leisure time activities. On the next blank, right-hand page in your notebook write the title, "Talents And Skills I Use in Leisure Time Activities," and compose your list (or use pages 47-48). Each leisure time activity included on your previous list should have a corresponding list of talents and skills.

↫ Step Seven ↬
Prioritizing Skills

The final step in the self discovery formula is to combine the talents and skills you identified in Steps Three, Four, Five, and Six. Carefully review the talents and skills you have listed (pages 32-35, 42-43, and 47-48). In your notebook, on the next blank, right-hand page write the title, "Prioritized Talents and Skills," or use page 49. Compare the talents

WHAT I LIKED ABOUT PAST JOBS

1. _____
   _____
   _____

2. _____
   _____
   _____

3. _____
   _____
   _____

4. _____
   _____
   _____

5. _____
   _____
   _____

6. _____
   _____
   _____

7. _____
   _____
   _____

WHAT I LIKED ABOUT PAST JOBS

8. _____

_____

_____

9. _____

_____

_____

10. _____

_____

_____

11. _____

_____

_____

12. _____

_____

_____

13. _____

_____

_____

14. _____

_____

_____

TALENTS & SKILLS USED DOING WHAT I LIKED

1. _____

_____

_____

2. _____

_____

_____

3. _____

_____

_____

4. _____

_____

_____

5. _____

_____

_____

6. _____

_____

_____

7. _____

_____

_____

TALENTS & SKILLS USED DOING WHAT I LIKED

8. _____

_____

_____

9. _____

_____

_____

10. _____

_____

_____

11. _____

_____

_____

12. _____

_____

_____

13. _____

_____

_____

14. _____

_____

_____

LEISURE TIME ACTIVITIES I ENJOY

1. _____
   _____
   _____

2. _____
   _____
   _____

3. _____
   _____
   _____

4. _____
   _____
   _____

5. _____
   _____
   _____

6. _____
   _____
   _____

7. _____
   _____
   _____

LEISURE TIME ACTIVITIES I ENJOY

8. _____
   _____
   _____

9. _____
   _____
   _____

10. _____
    _____
    _____

11. _____
    _____
    _____

12. _____
    _____
    _____

13. _____
    _____
    _____

14. _____
    _____
    _____

and skills from these four steps with each other. Then, prioritize your talents and skills so that the talent listed in the number one spot is your strongest skill (the one you most enjoy using). Number two should be your next strongest skill (next most enjoyable skill), etc.

When you've completed this prioritizing, you'll have a snapshot of who you are—and the talents you like to use. In other words:

You will know what you are best at and what you most enjoy doing.

You will begin to realize you are so much more than just a job title. You are more than a bus driver, a sales clerk, an accountant, or a lawyer. You are a unique and intricate collection of talents, skills, and traits. Once you decide how to use your uniqueness—you can make a difference in this world by doing the things you do best. When you use your natural talents on a regular basis, you will experience the satisfaction and self worth which is necessary to live a happy and healthy life. This is important, so I will repeat it:

You are much more than a job title. You are a unique and intricate collection of talents, skills, and traits. Once you decide how to use your uniqueness—you can make a difference in this world by doing the things you do best. When you use your natural talents on a regular basis, you will experience the satisfaction and self worth which is necessary to live a happy and healthy life.

By analyzing your successes rather than your failures, you have begun the process of recognizing your worth. The next step toward work happiness is determining what a job or career must give you in return.

TALENTS & SKILLS I USE
IN LEISURE TIME ACTIVITIES

1. _____
_____
_____

2. _____
_____
_____

3. _____
_____
_____

4. _____
_____
_____

5. _____
_____
_____

6. _____
_____
_____

7. _____
_____
_____

TALENTS & SKILLS I USE
IN LEISURE TIME ACTIVITIES

8. _____

_____

_____

9. _____

_____

_____

10. _____

_____

_____

11. _____

_____

_____

12. _____

_____

_____

13. _____

_____

_____

14. _____

_____

_____

PRIORITIZED TALENTS & SKILLS

1. _____

2. _____

3. _____

4. _____

5. _____

6. _____

7. _____

8. _____

9. _____

10. _____

11. _____

12. _____

13. _____

14. _____

15. _____

16. _____

17. _____

18. _____

2

Understanding Your Values

What is important to you as an individual? What beliefs guide your behavior? What do you look for in a job? What are your work values? Knowing your career values will help you understand *why* you do or don't enjoy your job. When you are clear about your values, you can make career choices that work.

Has there ever been a time in your life when you felt "out of sorts?" Things weren't going right, but you didn't know why? Oftentimes this frustration is caused because your values are not being met by what you are doing.

For example, the secretary to the president of a major corporation met with me recently. She was confused, dissatisfied, and very unhappy with her job. As we began our discussion, she said, "I don't understand why I feel the way I do. I have this great job working for the president. It's the highest admin-

50

istrative position in the company. I have all kinds of responsibility, authority, and challenge. Yet, I'm so unhappy. I have no idea why—and it's driving me crazy."

After some discussion, she determined that her talents and skills were being utilized fairly well, so that wasn't the cause of her unhappiness. However, as I helped her identify her values, the internal beliefs which were so important to her as an individual, she soon discovered the cause of her dilemma. Not *one* of her top five career values was being met by her job. No wonder she was discontent!

Like most of us, she wasn't even aware what her values actually were, much less how they could influence her job happiness. Once she had identified her career values and the role they played in her happiness, she could make some choices. She had the power to take action to change her situation; which she did. Now, she is extremely happy with her job.

I can make two guarantees—and they are not death and taxes. I guarantee that if your career values are *not* being met by your job, you will be unhappy with what you are doing. I also guarantee that if your top values *are* being met by your job, you will, in fact, enjoy what you are doing.

How many of your friends and coworkers became dissatisfied with their job, went out and found a new job, and were still unhappy? Sometimes, with a stroke of luck, a new job is the answer; but usually once the novelty wears off, a new job isn't any better than the old one. Why? Because, until a person identifies their career values, they won't be able to determine if a job is meeting those values.

Before you begin to discover your career values, let me give you some examples of work values other people have said are important to them. You might share some of these values, and you might not. You might have values which are not listed here. Everyone has their own

unique set of values. Your values will be different from mine, your friends'
and your coworkers'. There are no right or wrong values—only different ones.

Career Values

authority	freedom
creativity	honesty
personal growth	recognition
daytime work hours	large salary
family benefits	understanding boss
short commute time	large or small company
company loyalty	location
friendly co-workers	work privacy

Are you ready to discover your career values? Review the values listed
above and think about what a job must provide in order for you to
consider it a good job. Ask yourself, "What is the most important thing
I need to be happy in my work?" Realize, there are probably many
things you would *like* a job to offer. But, to start your list, determine
what is *the most important* thing you want in a job. That top requirement should go on line number one below the heading "Values: What I
Need To Be Happy" (see page 54).

Good. Now that you have determined your highest job priority, ask
yourself, "If a job meets my first requirement, what else must it offer for
me to be happy?" For instance, if your number one requirement is that
you work in Chicago (that's where you live and you won't consider
relocating for any job), what else do you need to be happy? Maybe it's
important for you to work for a small company; so that goes on the
second line. Then ask yourself, "If I work in Chicago for a small company, what else do I need?" You'd like a job to offer an opportunity for
personal growth. So, "personal growth" is added to your value list.
Then ask yourself, "If I work in Chicago, for a small company, and

there is opportunity for personal growth, what else do I need?" You need a competitive salary...and so on...until you have listed at least seven or eight values.

Pretty simple, right? On the next blank, right-hand page in your notebook write the title, "Values: What I Need To Be Happy." Write down your list of values in your notebook or use page 54.

Good job! I hope you're having fun with this. It's always exciting to work on the most important person in the world—**you**! At this point, you should have your career values written down. These are essential to your work happiness.

Even though you already asked yourself what is *most* important and what is *next* most important—it is quite likely that upon reflection, the priority of your values will change. Therefore, the next exercise is to create a more accurate picture of who you are by re-prioritizing your list of work values. This exercise will take some time—and thinking power—but it's well worth the effort. The rest of your life may be affected by the results of this labor. Remember, you are beginning to pour a rock-solid foundation on which to build your future.

Are you ready? To begin re-prioritizing your list of work values, you need to compare the value at the top of your "Values: What I Need To Be Happy." list with the second value to determine which is indeed most important to you. Whichever one is most important, compare it to the next value, and so forth, until you have gone through all of the values on your list. The item which survives as the most important value is your new number one value.

To see how this process works, let's return to our previous example. (Remember your work values were: working in Chicago, for a small company, offering personal growth, and a competitive salary. To make the list longer, let's add: training, a good boss, and daytime work hours.) To re-prioritize this list, you would have to ask yourself, "To be happy, is it more important that my job is located in Chicago or that I work for a small company?" Well, for many reasons, you need to stay in Chicago;

VALUES: WHAT I NEED TO BE HAPPY

1. _____

2. _____

3. _____

4. _____

5. _____

6. _____

7. _____

8. _____

9. _____

10. _____

11. _____

12. _____

13. _____

14. _____

15. _____

16. _____

17. _____

18. _____

but it would be okay to work for a large company. Therefore, working in Chicago is more important. Now, is it more important to work in Chicago or to have personal growth? Staying in Chicago is more important. Is staying in Chicago or a competitive salary more important? Staying in Chicago is still more important. Is working in Chicago or training more important? Staying in Chicago is more important. Is working in Chicago or having a good boss more important? Working in Chicago is more important. And, how does working during the day fare? After comparing all of your listed values, working in Chicago remains your number one value. This value should be written in the number one spot below the title, "Prioritized Values."

Continue with this analysis. Is it more important to work for a small company or to have personal growth opportunities? You really want to advance in your work, therefore personal growth is more important. Is personal growth or a competitive salary more important? Personal growth is more important than a competitive salary. What about training? Well, if you're offered training it would help you grow, so training is more important. Is training or a good boss more important? You've had difficult bosses before, they make life miserable. Therefore, a good boss is more important than training. Is a good boss or daytime work hours more important? A good boss is more important. So, even at this point, the order of your values has changed (see below).

Original top four values:	Top four re-prioritized values:
1. Work in Chicago	1. Work in Chicago
2. Small Company	2. Good Boss
3. Personal Growth	3. Training
4. Competitive Salary	4. Personal Growth

Next you need to compare working for a small company versus receiving a competitive salary and working daytime hours. A competitive salary is more important than working for a small company or working during the day, thus a competitive salary would be number five on your list. And, finally, is working for a small company or working during the day more important to you? Well, for a good, small company you wouldn't mind working a night shift, so small company is sixth on your list and working daytime hours is seventh.

Do you see how quickly the order of your values can change? Go ahead and review your list of values. On the next blank, right-hand page in your notebook after the title, "Prioritized Values," or on the following page, rewrite your values in their prioritized order.

Look at your list of prioritized values. Study them. They mean a lot to your future and to your happiness. Whatever you do in life, you should make certain that at least your top four or five values are met. It is your responsibility. (I will discuss later how you can assure that any future job will meet your values.)

Additionally, you can see how beneficial it would be for your supervisor (if you have one) to understand your values. If they knew what values you worked and lived by, they would be able to manage you accordingly. Likewise, if you understood your supervisor's values, communication and cooperation could dramatically improve between the two of you. Imagine, each of you would understand the other, and as a result, both of you would conceivably be much more productive and satisfied. Unfortunately, most employees and supervisors do not share this knowledge. It works like magic. Try it.

Remember, values affect the direction your life takes. You will never discover job satisfaction and fulfillment if you don't know, understand, and communicate your values. If your values aren't being satisfied, you aren't pursuing your mission in life. If you skipped the above exercise, go back and do it. Values are what drive you. You can't determine the career and job best suited for you unless you have this key piece of information.

I hope you're feeling energized. By doing these exercises you're getting to know yourself better and learning what motivates you. Aren't you curious about where and how you can use your skills to realize your greatest potential?

PRIORITIZED VALUES

1. _____

2. _____

3. _____

4. _____

5. _____

6. _____

7. _____

8. _____

9. _____

10. _____

11. _____

12. _____

13. _____

14. _____

15. _____

16. _____

17. _____

18. _____

3

What You're Meant To Do

Most people aren't aware of the skills they possess, much less what direction they want to go in life. Since you've invested the time and effort to identify, evaluate, and understand your skills and values, you have a sound basis for finding out what you're meant to do. The knowledge of who you are will point you towards a happy career and a healthy life.

By discovering your skills and values, you can determine what your personal niche might be, and you can look for the job that is right for you.

This process of self discovery is like putting a jigsaw puzzle together: you start out with lots of small pieces, and as the pieces start to go together, the puzzle becomes a little more whole.

You are constructing a puzzle of yourself. And, as with a jigsaw puzzle, the pieces don't automatically fall into position. Each piece must be worked until it fits into the rest of the puzzle. With each piece of information you gathered in Chapter 1, your understanding of who you are and what you can do became clearer, the picture became more whole.

You now know your talents, skills, and work values. Is your future beginning to take shape in your mind? You can't force it to happen; don't expect to snap your fingers and have a picture suddenly appear. But now that you recognize the skills you enjoy using most, and you know your career values, you can begin thinking about where and how you want to use your skills and talents.

For every set of talents and skills there is a profession and a job. Your goal is to find the opportunities that enhance who you are. It is exciting to anticipate the outcome—your whole life is being revitalized.

Your answers to the following questions will help you find the job which suits you best. For now, only read through the list. Don't write anything down. You can put your responses in writing later.

❑ What do you do with very little effort?

❑ Have you ever been so involved in an activity that you lost all track of time? If so, what were you doing?

❑ If you were guaranteed success, what would you do?

❑ What do people compliment you on?

❑ Would you like to switch jobs with someone? If yes, who and why?

❑ How would you describe a perfect day?

❑ What changes must you make in order to have more perfect days?

❑ What have you done which you felt really made a difference?

❑ What are some of your favorite memories?

❑ Of all that you do, which things are the most fun?

❑   Have you ever dreamt of doing something you've never done before? What was it?

By answering these questions, your inner desires will become clearer. Think about your responses *before* writing them down. You'll have fun answering the questions, and you'll enjoy reading and rereading your responses.

At the top of the next blank, right-hand page in your notebook write, "Thought Stimulating Questions" (or use pages 61-62). Rewrite each question from above, and then follow it with your answer.

If you are genuinely committed to improving your life, this is your chance. No longer must you settle for something you don't want to do.

You are the developer and the builder—you now have the knowledge and the tools to be in control of your future.

Take advantage of "me" time; the time to write and think about *you*. You deserve it. Your happiness depends on it.

Now that you've answered these thought provoking questions, at the top of the next several blank, right-hand pages in your notebook write, "Creative Thinking Notes" (or use pages 64-66). Pick a quiet place, somewhere you can be alone. Sit in a relaxed position and take twenty minutes to contemplate your future. Close your eyes. Relax. Enter a quiet, meditative state and ponder what you truly would like to do. As ideas cross your mind, immediately write them down in your notebook. It is imperative that you write your thoughts down as they come to you—most thoughts are fleeting and it would be impossible for you to remember all of them later.

After twenty minutes, close your notebook. Do not look at your notes. Then, a couple of days later, repeat this session. Make more notes. Repeat this exercise three or four times over a period of a couple of

THOUGHT STIMULATING QUESTIONS

What do you do with very little effort? _____

_____

_____

Have you ever been so involved in an activity that you lost all track
of time? If so, what were you doing? _____

_____

_____

If you were guaranteed success, what would you do? _____

_____

_____

What do people compliment you on? _____

_____

_____

Would you like to switch jobs with someone? If yes, who and why?

_____

_____

_____

How would you describe a perfect day? _____

_____

_____

_____

THOUGHT STIMULATING QUESTIONS

What changes must you make in order to have more perfect days?

_____

_____

_____

What have you done which you felt really made a difference? ____

_____

_____

_____

What are some of your favorite memories? _____

_____

_____

_____

Of all that you do, which things are the most fun? _____

_____

_____

_____

Have you ever dreamt of doing something you've never done before? What was it? _____

_____

_____

_____

weeks, and, only then, review your notes. Compare your thoughts from these sessions with your responses to the thought stimulating questions you answered earlier. Are there any similarities?

Now that the foundation is set, let's look at other strategies which will assist you as you continue to design your perfect life.

Job Success Formula
If you are using the talents and skills you enjoy, if your values are being met, and you feel as though you are making a difference; you will *love* your job.

CREATIVE THINKING NOTES

CREATIVE THINKING NOTES

CREATIVE THINKING NOTES

Part Two

Designing
Your Ideal Life

4

Acquiring
Valuable
Advice

B y completing the self discovery exercises in Part One, you've
set the foundation for your new career. What other pieces of
information can you gather which will help you build your future? The next step is what I call "Informational Interviewing," a technique of acquiring useful data from people by asking effective questions. The purpose of this step is to confirm that you're following the
right direction; you're gathering reinforcement before you plunge into
the job search scene.

In the first phase of Informational Interviewing you will recontact
the people who gave you advice earlier. Remember, you asked your
friends, relatives, and co-workers what they thought your strong points
were? Now, go back to them, to ask specific questions about the career
you're interested in.

Below is a simple, five-step **Communications Formula** you should follow each time you conduct an Informational Interview. This formula is succinct, yet very effective:

Communications Formula

1. Identify yourself and state why you are calling.
2. Explain your situation.
3. Tell the person about your skills and abilities.
4. Let them know your interests.
5. Ask for their advice.

Since last talking with these people, you have a better idea of where you will focus your job search energies. It is vital you share as much of this new information as possible with each person you interview. If they don't know enough about you or your needs, they will not be able to give you appropriate advice.

Think of it like this: If I wanted to take my wife out to dinner for our wedding anniversary, and I don't go to restaurants very often, I might call my friend, Jim, who eats out frequently. "Jim," I say, "I want to take my wife out to dinner. Where do you suggest we go?" Have I provided enough information to Jim so that he can give me good advice? No. He can't give me a valid suggestion.

However, if I say, "Jim, I want to take my wife out to dinner for our wedding anniversary. It's a special occasion, so I don't care what I spend. I don't mind driving an hour or so out of the city, although I'd prefer a smaller restaurant, with nice ambiance. Oh, my wife loves seafood; so that's important, too. Can you suggest a good restaurant?" Now Jim has enough information, and he can make an appropriate suggestion.

How do you handle an Informational Interview with a relative or friend? Remember what your purpose is: you are trying to determine how to best use the talents you possess. Below is an example of an introduction which follows the Communications Formula:

Hi, Jason, this is Tom Welch calling. I'd like to get your advice on some-

thing. Is this a convenient time? (Item one: you identified yourself and why you are calling.) *As you know, I've been doing a lot of thinking about my career lately...* (Item two: you explained your situation.) *...and I've discovered that my strengths are: interpersonal communication, organization, persuasion skills, and decision making abilities.* (Item three: you presented your skills.) *I've been thinking about getting into sales.* (Item four: you stated what your interest is.) *If you were me and you had these skills, what would you do? Do you have any suggestions or ideas?* (Item five: you asked for their advice.)

Here is the introduction again, without interruption:

Hi, Jason. This is Tom Welch calling. I'd like to get your advice on something. Is this a convenient time? As you know, I've been doing a lot of thinking about my career lately and I've discovered that my strengths are: interpersonal communication, organization, persuasion skills, and decision making abilities. I've been thinking about getting into sales. If you were me and had these skills, what would you do? Do you have any suggestions or ideas?

Pretty easy, right? The key to a productive interview is to provide sufficient information about yourself so the person you are interviewing can give appropriate advice.

What? The above example doesn't exactly fit your situation? No problem. Maybe you're not sure what your interests are or what you want to do. With a slight adjustment to your introduction, you can still gather helpful information:

...I've discovered that my strengths are interpersonal communication, organization, persuasion skills, and decision making abilities. However, I'm not sure how to best use these skills. You know me pretty well. Do you have any ideas or suggestions?

The opinions and advice you receive during these interviews will be extremely valuable. Relatives, friends, and co-workers see you more *objectively* than you see yourself. So, before starting your series of Informational Interviews, dedicate a section in your notebook to the responses you receive. Take copious notes during each conversation, as this constructive and objective data will further clarify your career options.

PHASE ONE-INFORMATIONAL INTERVIEWS

Date/Time of Interview: _____

Name of Person: _____

Telephone Number: _____

Notes: _____

_____

_____

_____

_____

After conducting these interviews, you should have a better idea of the changes you must make in order to pursue career satisfaction and life fulfillment. Maybe you can make your current job and career work for you—or maybe you can't. The possibilities are as individual as you are. So, don't be discouraged. Even the seemingly most difficult situation has a solution. I promise.

Cross Transferring Skills

If the results of the exercises in Part One and the information you received in phase one of your Informational Interviews point you toward a profession quite different from the one you're working in now, don't be alarmed or afraid. In some cases, additional education will be required; either specialized training or another degree. However, with over 30,000 different jobs, and many of them requiring the same skills and talents, there are many opportunities for you to enter a new profession by simply **cross transferring** your skills.

An example of someone who successfully cross transferred their skills is Susan, a woman who was referred to me several years ago.

When we met, Susan had worked as a secretary for the last twelve years. She felt burnt out. "Okay," I said, "if you're tired of your job, what do you want to do next?"

She thought for a minute, and then responded, "Well, I guess I'll be a secretary at another company."

"You sure sound excited about doing that again," I said.

"Well, it's all I know," she retorted. "It's all I've ever done."

"Okay," I continued. "What do you *like* to do? Is there anything you *really* enjoy doing?"

"I can't think of anything in particular...oh, there is *one* thing I like—but it wouldn't make any difference."

"Let's try it," I said. "What is it?"

"I like weddings. I like everything about weddings," she replied. "People are so happy. It's a festive occasion, there is so much to it: invitations, gifts, food, receptions, and music...I just really like weddings."

"Well," I said, "two things come to mind. You could either get married a lot—."

"No!" she interrupted. "That's not the answer."

"...or you could work at a business involved with weddings, like a bridal shop," I suggested.

"That would be great fun, but I don't have any experience. No one would hire me."

"Let's think about this," I encouraged. "Tell me a little bit more about what you did as a secretary."

"Well, I was on the phone a lot, coordinating calls for my boss and making arrangements for meetings, et cetera," Susan began. "Also, I had to keep my boss organized—he was a mess. I had to meet and greet people. I had to interact with other executives in the company, to make sure certain things happened on time. I also did quite a bit of correspondence and scheduling."

I thought and said, "You did a lot of things, didn't you? Your duties involved organizing information, right?"

"Oh yeah, lots of that."

"And scheduling?"

"Yes."

"And interaction with people?"

"Yes."

"And communication skills?" I continued.

"Definitely."

"So," I reviewed, "organization, coordination, scheduling and communications—sounds like many of the skills that a bridal consultant would use."

"Well, when you look at it that way, I guess you're right!" she said hopefully.

"I'll tell you what, Susan. Why don't you look in the yellow pages under 'Bridal Shops' and telephone some of the stores. Talk with the owners and tell them about the skills you have; and how you love weddings. Get their advice on where you might best fit in their industry."

Susan went home and followed my instructions. After only a few telephone calls, one of the bridal shop owners said, "I need someone like you. Can you be here at four o'clock this afternoon?"

When Susan arrived at the shop for her interview, she talked in depth about her skills. She bubbled with enthusiasm over the wedding industry, and she also demonstrated how her skills could add *value* to the business. Rather than just state that she was organized, Susan discussed specific examples of things she had accomplished which demonstrated her organizational abilities.

Before Susan walked out of his door, she had received a job offer!

Today, she is still working at the bridal shop—which, really for her is not a job, it's a love, a *passion*. Believe me, Susan does not have trouble jumping out of bed in the morning to go to work.

What gave Susan the **power** to switch careers? The knowledge of her skills—and the fact that most skills are cross transferable between professions. Yours are, too.

Let's review what Susan did. First, she understood her skills well enough to talk intelligently about them. Second, she identified an industry which was of interest to her. Third, she contacted people in the industry to ask for their advice on how and where her skills might best be used in the industry.

In order to successfully cross transfer your skills into a new career, you must:

❑ understand your strengths

❑ know what skills are necessary in the profession of interest to you

❑ convince someone, through evidence of what you've accomplished in the past, that you can successfully use your skills on their behalf

Realize, "on their behalf" means being able to solve a problem they have or to add value to their business. The often-tried approach, "Hey, I'm a great person with lots of talent. I learn fast, so you should hire me" doesn't work. However, when you demonstrate a match between someone else's needs and your skills—then you'll make progress.

> ## Employers hire people for two reasons:
> 1. to solve a problem, and
> 2. to add value to their business.

Let's assume you've selected an industry which is of interest to you, and you don't have much (if any) experience in the industry. Your next step would be to talk with people in the industry. After all, what better way to obtain information on an industry, than talking with someone who is a part of it? With this step, you are taking your information gathering skills to another level. You are researching data that will help you greatly when you begin your job search.

In the second phase of Informational Interviewing you will seek advice from people within the industry you want to enter, from people who are doing what you want to do.

First, compile a list of companies in the industry (the yellow pages, library, and chamber of commerce are great sources for business lists). If you know someone who works at one of the companies, use them as your contact. If you don't know anyone who works there, contact a department which is accustomed to dealing with the public. For instance, someone who works in customer service, marketing and sales, public relations, or even accounts payable and receivable, would most likely be able to point you in the right direction. (Typically, the higher you go in an organization, the better the information you'll receive.) Remember, most people will be happy to give you their opinion and advice.

In this telephone campaign, you will use the same approach as in Phase One:

Communications Formula

1. Identify yourself and state why you are calling.
2. Explain your situation.
3. Tell the person about your skills and abilities.
4. Let them know your interests.
5. Ask for their advice. Where would your skills best fit in the industry?

Again, you will want to make notes of your conversations. At the top of the next blank, right-hand page in your notebook write, "Phase Two-Informational Interviews."

Your telephone introduction might sound like this:

"Hello. Bill? This is John Smith. I'm telephoning you for some advice on the insurance industry. Is this a convenient time? I've been involved in furniture sales for the past ten years and recently had an opportunity to evaluate my talents and skills. My strengths are: determination, a belief in myself, a desire to help others improve their lives, and good communication and organizational skills. I'm fascinated by the insurance industry and would love to become a part of it. In that I have a degree in business and ten years of experience, where do you see the best place for me in the insurance industry?"

Listen to his advice. Discuss it if necessary, and then thank Bill for his time. Finally, ask one more question:

"Is there anyone else in your company, or elsewhere in the industry, who you feel might have some advice for me or might be able to point me in the right direction?"

The answer to this final question will help you develop a list of contacts within the industry you desire to enter.

After you've made several calls and are feeling more comfortable with this approach, you should consider expanding the scope of your questioning. Consider this: if, through your interviews, you become aware of some problems within the industry—and you are able to de-

---

PHASE TWO-INFORMATIONAL INTERVIEWS

Date/Time of Interview: _____

Name of Person: _____

Telephone Number: _____

Notes: _____

_____

_____

_____

_____

vise solutions to the problems—you would then stand out from the crowd of other job applicants. You could become a valuable asset for a future employer. Remember, there are only two reasons why employers hire people: to solve a problem or to add value to their business.

It is vital for you to understand what's going on in the industry you wish to enter. By simply expanding the scope of your questions, you will begin to extract valuable information from the people you speak with. Since most people enjoy talking about themselves, give them the opportunity to do just that. After they have given you their advice on where your skills might best be utilized, casually ask: *"How did you get involved in this industry? What do you like about it? What bothers you about it?"*

When they tell you what they don't like about the business, it is the same as if they were telling you the industry's problems. If several contacts within the same industry mention similar problems, you have acquired valuable ammunition; ammunition which you can use later in the course of your job search.

Caution: when doing your Informational Interviews, use discretion. Not everyone you telephone will open up to you—nor will everyone have an abundance of time to spend on the phone. If you have developed a rapport and the person seems to have time for a discussion, take advantage of it. If, however, they sound rushed and anxious to get off the phone, ask if there is a more convenient time for you to call them back.

Not only will these Informational Interviews be an invaluable source of rich information, they will oftentimes spark creative ideas for you to use to your benefit.

As you continue on your journey to revitalize your career, remember what your goals are: to live a happier and healthier life. When you enjoy your career—your life's work—you will encounter a feeling of security unlike any you've experienced before. You see, other people can ask you to perform a task, and they can assign you a goal; but no one can give you a *passion*. Passion comes from inside you; it is the *real* you, it is *your* desire.

Do you recognize the name Dennis Byrd? He was a defensive lineman for the New York Jets in the 1980s. During a football game, he was severely injured. Immediately following the accident, he was paralyzed from the neck down. The day after sustaining the injury, his wife brought their two year old daughter to the hospital to visit Dennis. As his nurse lifted the little girl onto his chest, so she could give her daddy a hug, Dennis said, "You know, the accident took away my ability to move my arms and legs, but it can't take away the fact that I'm your daddy."

You see, while lying in the hospital bed, contemplating his future, Dennis realized something very important:

No one can take away who you are; not your talents and certainly not your passion.

What is *your* passion? Declare your mission—and then live it!

5

Creating
Your Mission
Statement

Why are you special? What can you do better than anyone else? Remember, you are not merely a job title. You are so much more than a marketing manager, a grocery store clerk, an auto worker, or a vice president. You are a unique combination of talents, skills, and values—and you can make a difference in this world by doing the things you do best.

Leave your past behind. Don't be crippled by fear of the unknown. Focus on what is really you. What talents and skills can you offer? What problems can you solve? Where can you best add value?

Review the notes you've already made. Read your list of talents. Contemplate your list of prioritized values. What material did you gather during the Informational Interviews? At this point in your search, you should be ready to lock in on your dreams and to set a goal, to declare your mission your *passion*.

After deep soul searching, which you have done if you've completed the exercises in this book, you should know what you really want to do. (Even if you've had a hunch all along, of what was right for you, *now* you should be more certain.) Your newly-acquired knowledge should give you strength. It is time for action.

Declaring what you are meant to do is a journey through the mind and heart. You are the one who must make the journey; you are the navigator.

To help you remain on course, it is very important for you to have a mission statement. This mission statement is your vision—your goal. It is a declaration of your purpose in life—what type of work will bring you the most satisfaction—and it will guide you to a healthier life-style.

As an example of a mission statement, here is mine:

> Through the effective use of reasoning, communication, and persuasion skills, I provide ideas and solutions to help others attain personal abundance in their life work and their lives. I make living more exciting and fun.

At the top of the next blank, right-hand page in your notebook write, "Mission Statement" (or use the space on the following page). Give careful consideration to the words you choose. This statement will help you navigate the most exciting road of your life.

Read your Mission Statement daily. In order for you to realize success, you must *believe* you can make your goal happen. If you don't have a genuine belief in your mission, you will lose your motivation to act. To prevent this from happening, I will show you how to develop a winning belief system that is so enduring that nothing will prevent you from reaching your dream.

MY MISSION STATEMENT

_____

_____

_____

_____

_____

_____

_____

_____

_____

_____

_____

_____

_____

_____

_____

_____

_____

_____

_____

_____

_____

_____

_____

_____

6

Developing A Winning Belief System

A selection of top producing sales people in the country were recently asked: "To what do you attribute your success?" Their number one response was: belief. They believed in themselves and the products they sold. (To participate in the survey, they had to earn a minimum of $250,000 a year.) These sales people reinforced a very important *life truth*:

With a deep commitment to who you are and what you can do, you will succeed in whatever you attempt.

In other words, before you can improve your life, your emotions and beliefs must be working *for* you, *not* against you.

Webster defines *belief* as "confidence or trust." Your beliefs are the foundation on which your life is built. They control your actions and emotions. Your behavior is greatly influenced by your beliefs; and the stronger your beliefs, the more purposefully you will act.

Let's take this one step further. Since your job demands so much of your time and thought—so much of *you*—any belief or feeling you have about your job greatly influences other parts of your life. If you felt positive about your work, those feelings could be transferred into other areas of your life. Therefore, if you could at least gain control of the feelings you have about your job, you'd then have far greater control of how you viewed other aspects of your life.

So much of a person's self-worth is influenced by their feelings about their job. How did it happen—that our identities became so intricately molded by our job titles and our professions? Unfortunately, this phenomena is caused by the erroneous belief in our society that: you are your job!

Recently, I attended a fortieth birthday party. As the guests stood around and talked, inevitably the conversation turned to "What do you do?" (Doesn't it always?)

One gentleman went into considerable detail about his management position at a restaurant. He discussed how the owners were marketing the restaurant, how sales were increasing, the selection of menu items, how the restaurant was attracting a greater lunch crowd, and on and on and on. Later in the evening, he pulled me aside and said he had overheard a conversation about my expertise in the career field. "Did you hear all of the things I said about the restaurant?" he asked me. "Well, I don't work there anymore. I was laid off a couple of weeks ago because business was slow. Do you think you could help me?"

He was too embarrassed to tell the truth among his peers. "As a matter-of-fact," he said, "I had to promise my wife that I wouldn't talk about my lay off or else she wouldn't come to the party." Both he and his wife were ashamed because of the **stigma attached to a job**.

Have you ever felt that way? I think all of us have at one time or another. It is a pity that such an erroneous belief of society causes such anguish and anxiety.

Who controls your thinking? Your believing? Your actions? You do! No one but yourself. Therefore, to change your emotions, to change your actions, you simply need to begin changing your beliefs. Start with this one belief: **you are more than a job title**.

By altering your beliefs, change will enter your life and your life can improve. The greatest resource you have is the power to change your attitude towards something. Abraham Lincoln once said, "Most folks are about as happy as they make up their minds to be."

In other words, you are in control of your happiness, and every other feeling and emotion you possess. Once you realize this, then you can alter any aspect of your life.

Too many people wait for someone else to change their beliefs and emotions for them. They hope someone else (employer, spouse, friend, or counselor) will make them feel better. When you expect another person to be the solution, you **dis-empower** yourself. And, while you wait for them, your energy drains away, along with your enthusiasm and self-confidence.

I was recently asked to speak to a group of employees who had been notified that the plant they worked at would be closing in six months. When I entered the conference room, I could sense their anger and hostility (towards the company, not me). My mission was to help these people realize the negative impact their anger was having on their lives—and the power they would gain once *they* made the decision to let go of their anger and allow positive beliefs into their lives. If they chose to think positively about the plant's closure, they would be **empowered** to go on with their lives. No longer would they fear the future, rather they would be excited about the journey ahead of them. Here is a brief excerpt of my presentation to them:

Life will change as soon as you decide you're going to do something different. If you say today, "You know, I'm really angry at this company. I feel betrayed. The management let me down. I worked here for twenty-three years, I didn't miss a day of work, I was never late—and I'm the first one to go! After all that time, wouldn't you think they'd have more respect for me? But NO, I'm out the door."

The longer you think like that, the louder you complain, and the more you hear everyone else around you complain, your morale will remain low and your attitude will deteriorate. But, as soon as you say, "Hey, every time I've gone out to find a new opportunity, my life has been better. I'm glad this happened." Now, you've chosen to thinking positively, and you are empowered to deal with the opportunity at hand.

Successful people have been studied, and one of the traits they share is an overwhelming belief that everything in life happens for a reason; and they make the reason work for them. Successful people take a situation, let's say it's the closing of this place, they take a monumental problem which consumes their thinking, and they can shrink it—mentally shrink the problem—and move it to the back of their minds, so that pretty soon what's in the forefront of their thought is "What's next? What can I do that's different? How will I be happy?"

On the other hand, less successful people take a problem, and rather than shrink it, they activate it until it gets bigger and bigger and bigger. They let it consume their thinking, even if there is nothing they can do about it. You cannot stop this plant from closing—it is beyond your control. So, instead of allowing negative feelings to consume you, why not think positively?

Who was being hurt by this anger? Whose lives were being blocked by negative beliefs?

Does *your* belief system continually permit anger to invade your thoughts? Do you believe your parents guided you into the wrong field, and that makes you angry? Do you believe a counselor was at fault for suggesting an inappropriate major, and that makes you angry? Do you believe your boss is at fault for not promoting you (or for firing you), and that makes you angry? Again, who is hampered by your anger? Not your parents. Not the counselor. Not your boss. Only you.

Are you angry at yourself for failing to make changes in your life? Even this belief, which causes anger, is hurting you. Negative beliefs and feelings (which limit your actions) hinder your progress toward a better quality of life, just as positive beliefs and feelings are empowering. They spur you to action.

What you believe is your choice—you design your world. You can choose the way you look at anything in life.

How can you use this power to revitalize your thinking and your behavior? One way is to genuinely listen to your "self-talk," the little voice inside your head. What does this inner voice say to you? What does it reveal about your beliefs? Has your voice ever said:

- ❑ "Why should I even think about improving my life? I'll never be able to do it."

- ❑ "What a stupid thing I did. I'm probably not as good as other people who are also looking for a job."

- ❑ "What if no other company hires me? Maybe I shouldn't risk looking for another job."

- ❑ "What if my skills are so rusty, I can't do the job any more? I better stay where I am, even though I'm so unhappy."

These negative thoughts and beliefs only lower self-esteem. Do they spur you to action? On the contrary. Just reading them makes you feel smaller and less significant.

What you think about yourself affects how you act toward yourself and others. You see, your subconscious is like a sponge; it believes what you tell it. Your action—and lack of action—is governed by your beliefs.

The first step in creating a winning belief system is to **listen to your self-talk**. If you discover negative internal conversation, concentrate on ending it and replacing it with positive thought. Ask yourself positive questions; questions which require positive answers. For instance, you might say, "How can this anger, this disappointment, this fear, be used as a springboard for me to change my life? Are my lack of promotions or my meager salary a signal that I've gone as far as I can in this organization? I'm unhappy here, maybe this is the perfect time to take *control* of my life and make things happen. I have the power to change. A change would make me feel better, more confident."

Instead of continuously going over mistakes in your mind, think about actions and results; what you can **do** to create a better future.

If your inner voice tells you that you hate to get out of bed each morning because you dislike your job, begin telling yourself, "Since I now know my talents and I've prioritized my work values, I'm prepared to take action to change jobs." As you make this subtle change, from negative to positive beliefs, it will get easier for you to get up in the morning, because you have a goal: to apply the power of your knowledge toward a new career and a better job.

Talk to yourself about the life you want. Remember, when you believe something is true, you begin acting like it is true. For example, even if you dislike your current job or profession, and your dissatisfaction with your job is making your life miserable, the simple act of deciding to take control of your career will markedly improve your attitude. Your self-talk will say, "I'm so enthused I decided to take control.

This is an exciting journey. It's the best thing I've ever decided to do—for me."

When you change your internal conversation to positive talk, prepare yourself for renewed vitality and enthusiasm. Have you ever owned a rechargeable flashlight? When the battery begins to run low, the light dims. But after a night of recharging the battery, the light brightens again. Positive self-talk is your super charger. Your batteries will never be low again. The better you feel about yourself, and the more you believe in yourself, the more likely it is you will find happiness and success.

The second step to creating a winning belief system is to **trade one feeling for another**. You might turn the *anger* you feel (towards your employer, counselor, parents, etc.) into *excitement* (for the changes you are about to make in your job). The anger you feel can move you to action—and that's exciting. You've traded one feeling for another. Who controls your feelings? You do. Who benefits from them? You do. Would you rather feel negative (angry) or positive (excited)? Tell yourself, "I'm glad I got so mad about this, because now I'm going to do something. I'm finally going to take action and get some new results."

A friend of mine, who is a therapist, once told me that when any of his patients say they have a problem, the first thing he has them do is to trade the word "project" for the word "problem." Then he tells them to talk about their project. He has received tremendous results by having his patients simply change their terminology. You can do the same, by trading one emotion (feeling) for another.

Has your job or career ever frustrated you? What if you turned your frustration into enthusiasm for a change or a new beginning? Rather than tell yourself, "I'm so frustrated that I was passed over for a promotion again. When will management ever appreciate me?" Say, "I do a great job, and since this management doesn't recognize my abilities, I'm ready to find a company that will. It's really good this happened, because it has moved me into action. I haven't felt this enthused and excited in years." The change in your feelings, from frustration to en-thusiasm, will produce action.

Another example that shows the power your beliefs have over your actions is the following incident:

> A marketing manager for one of my corporate clients had been fired. When I met with him the day after he was notified of his termination, I asked him, "What was the toughest part of yesterday?"

> "The hardest thing was telling my family," he said. "I told them at dinner, and it was so difficult because my two daughters had never known their daddy to fail before."

> "Did you fail?" I asked.

> "I must have," he replied. "My company doesn't want me anymore."

> "Tell me a little bit about what you did over the past two years, while you were with the company," I requested.

> He explained that this was his first job in marketing, and he felt he had done a respectable job for the company. Prior to joining this firm, he had worked in engineering for another company. However, after experiencing several major accomplishments with this company, he realized he loved the world of marketing. And the customers really liked him.

> "Do you wish you were still in engineering?" I asked.

> "Oh no," he said. "Being able to gain experience in marketing was a tremendous benefit."

> "So, what's next?" I asked.

> "There's no doubt I'm going to stay in marketing," he replied. "I love it and I'm good at it."

> "So," I summarized, "the last two years gave you the opportunity to acquire experience in marketing, you discovered that you love it, and you're good at it—all at the same time?"

"Yes," he said.

"You didn't fail," I told him. "What you learned is priceless. These last two years have been a gold mine to you."

He sat back in his chair and began shaking his head. "You know, Tom, when you put it that way, you're absolutely right! I'm going back home and I will retell my story to my family. I know they'll feel better. I do."

All he did was changed his view (belief) of what had happened. He turned his frustration and feelings of failure into excitement for the future and feelings of success. As you begin cleansing yourself of disempowering beliefs, and welcoming winning beliefs, you too, will feel more accomplished. As you begin to change, you must concentrate on staying focused and committed to your new thought patterns.

If you notice negative feelings creeping into your thoughts, turn the negative into a positive or trade one word for another. No matter what happens in your life, ask yourself, "How can I benefit or learn from this event?"

Remember, you have the control. Trust yourself. No one else can dictate how you feel about anything.

Always use your emotions and beliefs in a way which will help you. Athletes call this thought control "being in the zone." They put themselves in a top mental state before a game. Imagine how much more effective you will be in your career if you are "in the zone," in a peak state of mind which only you can create. Think about the enthusiasm you could exude if you were doing something you loved to do—and your winning belief system was continuously keeping you in a feel-good emotional state. You only have one life to live, so live it well.

The third step to create a winning belief system is **at the end of each night, think about the things you did during the day which made you feel good**. They don't have to be big things; any small act you did or positive thing you said is appropriate. As you sleep, your subconscious will reflect on these activities, and when you wake up the next morning, you'll start a new day with enthusiasm.

Again, here are the key points to remember:

1. How you feel about any event is based upon your belief system, because this is what controls your emotions.

2. You have the ability to manage your beliefs and emotions through: perfecting positive self-talk, trading one emotion or feeling for another.

3. Ending each day by recognizing the good you've accomplished.

So far, you've acquired a lot of power to revitalize your career. However, studies have shown that at the beginning of a transition, people experience a lack of confidence and anxiety; they fear the unknown. How well you work through these emotions will determine your success.

Fear can bring a halt to the best plans. Therefore, the next strategy you will learn is how to overcome your fears—and to use the energy produced by fear to move you in your desired direction.

7

Overcoming The Fear Of Change

One hot and steamy summer day, as I was floating on an inner tube in the Ichetucknee River in North Central Florida, I realized one thing was missing: control. As I floated on the tube, with the river's current taking me wherever and however it chose, I thought, "This is how too many people manage their careers. They accept whatever comes along, letting their jobs and careers control their lives. They are 'floaters,' never asking themselves planning questions, such as: 'Is my job taking me in the direction I want to go?' 'Do I have a career goal?' 'What is important to me in life?' 'What role does my career play?'" Instead of taking the initiative, these people choose to ride life's currents. They complain, yet never take control to improve their situations.

Why are some people so passive? Usually, it is because they fear change.

> Fear is a signal that you're making progress.

The fear of change immobilizes them to the point that they believe they are powerless—and they give up—they relinquish control.

Do you look forward to change? Most people don't; especially when it involves their employment. I strongly believe that only one in five disenchanted workers would even consider *looking* for another job, because their fear of any change in their employment situation is so great. They are afraid to take chances.

The good news is you can acknowledge your fear, understand it, and then use it to your advantage. Successful people actually welcome change. They aren't afraid to make mistakes. They know that confronting their fears has forced them to grow, to mature. If they had avoided new situations; they would not have the knowledge and experience they have today.

The heart of life is change. To improve your life, you must not only accept change, you must welcome it. As "The Magic School Bus," a popular children's television program promotes, "Take chances. Make mistakes." If you continually strive to avoid changes in your life—you are doomed to sameness. When your life stays the same, you stagnate. The more you stagnate, the more your spirit dies...and you will be doomed to a form of living death.

How does your belief system produce fear in the first place? You become afraid when you live in the *future* instead of the *present*. Your thinking is controlled by what *might* happen.

Let go of the past. It does not exist; only your beliefs, based on your past experiences, remain with you. What drives your life is the energy of the present.

No matter how well you understand your talents, skills, and values; no matter how precisely you have determined which career or profession you want to pursue, if the fear of change prevents you from taking action, you will never pursue your mission. If fear causes you to associate pain with action, you are doomed to your present, dissatisfied state. (I know that is not the life you want, because you are reading this book.)

> Acknowledge your fear,
> understand it, and
> then use it to your advantage.

Types of Fear

Let's look at the different fears you may encounter whenever you contemplate change. Then, I'll discuss how you can use the energy produced by these fears to accept and initiate exciting changes in your life.

1. Fear of the unknown.
You're not sure how change will affect your life. What should you expect? Will it be good or bad? The uncertainty causes you to procrastinate (at best) or do nothing (at worst).

2. Fear of failure.
Instead of thinking positively about change, you focus on the negative: "What if I don't know how to find the right job?" "What if I do it wrong?" "What if I can't find another opportunity?" "What if no one really wants me?" So, you do nothing.

3. Fear of rejection.
Instead of acknowledging the fact that rejection comes with any job search and arming yourself with self-confidence, you concentrate on all of the obstacles which might get in your way: "What will my family think? What if they don't approve?" "What if I continuously get turned

down by employers?" "What if I'm not good enough or young enough or old enough for the job?" "What will my friends think? What if they think I'm doing something foolish?" "What if I'm not offered a comparable salary?" You can't possibly handle this much rejection, so you do nothing.

4. Fear of goals.
Although this fear is less obvious, it is very real. Some people are afraid to discover what their passion is, because once they have identified their passion, they would feel compelled to act upon it. However, if they don't know what their passion is, they remain unenlightened—and do nothing.

5. Fear of success.
Yes, there is a fear of success! Does your inner voice say, "Will my friends abandon me if I succeed? Will they avoid me if I've achieved recognition for my work?" "Will I become a workaholic if I'm too successful?" Rather than anticipate the glory of success, some people dwell only on the possible negative consequences—and do nothing.

Accepting Fear And Change

What scares you when you think about changes in your employment situation? The more attached you become to what you do today and what you are today, the more fear you'll experience when you anticipate tomorrow. Are you attached to your self-image as a truck driver, a carpenter or an accountant? Can you let go of this image and dream of your future?

Let fear be your friend. Fear is a signal that you're on the right track—you're making progress. Use fear as an asset. It can give you the energy to move forward in a focused direction and help you move beyond what you are comfortable with today. Nothing new begins until something old ends.

In the 1960s, one of the best goalies in the National Hockey League was Glen Hall, who played for the Chicago BlackHawks. He had years of experience and had played in hundreds of hockey games, many under tremendous pressure. Yet, even with all of that experience, he still felt sick to his stomach before the start of each game. He attributed his stomach sickness to a certain amount of fear he felt before any new challenge. However, rather than letting his fear paralyze him, he used it to his advantage—he used the energy it gave him to become one of the best goalies ever.

Fear can be a great motivator—or an inhibitor. You must decide how you will let fear work for you.

I once counseled Tito, a young man from Spain. He came to me for help in confronting his fear of entering the work force:

Tito had accomplished much in his young life. When he arrived in the United States, at the beginning of his junior year in high school, he didn't know the English language very well nor had he ever lived away from his home. He conquered English and overcame all of the cultural differences to graduate from high school with a 3.0 grade point average. He then went on to college, where he succeeded; finishing a degree which took most students five years to complete, in only three-and-a-half years.

Tito was now ready to start his career. But despite all he had accomplished, he was overcome with fear. He was afraid to look for a job. He knew he had to move beyond his education; but he feared rejection. He doubted if he could cope in the working world.

"Tito," I asked, "do you want to get rid of your fears?"

"Of course," he said.

"What if I told you there were no rejections, mistakes or failures? What if I replaced the words 'rejection,' 'mistake,' and 'failure' with the word 'result?' You do something (you take action) and you get a result. There are no mistakes or failures; only results. Simple, right? Now, *maybe* the result you get is not the one you wanted, so to get a different result, what do you have to do, Tito?"

"Change my action?" he answered.

"Exactly! And, what if the new action still doesn't produce the result you want?" I continued. "Could you change your action again, to get yet another result?"

"Yes, and once my actions produce the result I want, I then know what actions to follow the next time I want to achieve the same result," he concluded.

The lesson Tito learned: there are no mistakes or failures; only results.

Strategies to Learn

Here are some strategies you can use to accept fear into your life and to initiate change:

1. View change positively.

Remember in my discussion of beliefs, I stated that nothing in life has any meaning by itself. The only meaning it has is whatever meaning you attach to it. Let me give you an example:

> You're at home on a Saturday, and it begins to rain. You wanted to spend the day outdoors, but the weather has ruined your plans. You become angry, frustrated, and bored because you can't go outside.

The following Saturday, you plan to clean the inside of your house and to rearrange all of the furniture. It rains again, but this time you're happy, because you had already planned to work inside. You actually feel content.

Different emotions were caused by the same event: rain on Saturday. But based on your view of the situation, your emotions were totally different each day. One week the rain was bad; the next it was good. Change is much the same. You *know* changes will occur, they are a part of life. Why not alter your perspective of each situation as it happens?

You could use one of the techniques we discussed previously: trade the word "change" for the word "adventure." Although you tend to rebel against change, you might react more positively to an adventure. This might sound like oversimplifying, but remember, your subconscious does not make distinctions. It accepts what you tell it. If you tell your subconscious you're going on an adventure, your behavior will be more in tune with your true desires; the desire to take action, to grow, and to do something different than you've done before.

2. Ask yourself positive questions about change.

As you contemplate changes in your work and life, you need to ask yourself questions which focus on how you can make the change work to your *benefit* instead of focusing on how it might cause you *pain*. For instance: "How will this change help me grow?" "How will it make me a better person?" "If I change my career, how will my enthusiasm for life increase?" "What value will *my* talents and skills bring to others?"

I strongly suggest that you write each of these questions on a small piece of paper, and carry it with you. There will be days when the fear of change tries to creep back into your life, immobilizing you. If and when this happens, pull out the paper and answer the questions again. This exercise will help you remain focused on your goal, while renewing your excitement about your adventure.

> At a recent presentation, I spoke with a man who had lost his job the day before. Under the circumstances, I was amazed by his optimism. I was even more impressed by this man's positive attitude after he told me that two weeks ago his car was totalled when someone ignored a stop sign and hit his car; and that only one week ago his daughter was hit by a car travelling thirty-five miles per hour.

> The man explained that he expected the third blow, losing his job, because he had heard that bad things happened in sets of three. So, rather than feel defeated, he viewed these situations as challenges. As he stood in front of the room, he explained, "You never know what will happen. Everything happens for a reason. Only time will tell you why."

Needless to say, he was an inspiration to everyone, particularly those people who were feeling sorry for themselves. This man did not let the fear of change conquer him. He did not let major dilemmas override his belief that things happen for a reason. Circumstances forced him to make changes in his life, but he viewed these circumstances as *opportunities*, not as events to be feared.

Many people have prospered far beyond their expectations after dealing with unplanned occurrences. Once they dealt with each change, they realized an increase in self-esteem, wealth, and happiness; because they were in control of their lives. Even your current problem may be the best thing that ever happened to you. Consider how this man dealt with the loss of his job:

> One morning, John was fired from his job as vice president of engineering. He honestly felt it was the worst thing that could have happened to him, at the worst time in his life.

> However, the next day, as John sat in my office, he said,

"Tom, I didn't realize this until now...the last time I played softball was five years ago. I haven't coached my kids' teams for five years. I just took my son to college—he grew up, he's gone, and I've lost him. My daughter is in high school. I am so glad that these chains (stress, long hours, working Saturdays, working Sundays) have been cut. I can now go through high school with my daughter. I can go to her plays, watch her football games, whatever. I can do these things again. I lost the last five years of my life because I was so wrapped up in my career. Now, I *know* my firing was a blessing. It is the *best* thing that could have happened to me!"

Luckily, for John, he realized that his past did not equal his future. He understood that everything happens for a purpose and every negative experience—or *perceived* negative experience—can be the beginning of something better. To come to his realization, John asked himself positive questions, and his answers changed his beliefs, his emotions, and his attitude toward the future.

3. Realize change is a *will* not a *should*.

Pay attention to the *shoulds* in your life. At a minimum, they cause guilt; at a maximum, they can control your behavior. Right now, think about two things which you *should* do. Okay. Do you have them? (Was it difficult to focus on only two?) Now, do these *shoulds* stand between you and action, between you and life revitalization?

For instance: "I *should* think about how I can better use my skills." "I *should* figure out why I'm not happy in my job." "I *should* look for a new opportunity."

In order to produce action, you must change the *shoulds* to *wills*: "I *will* think about how I can better use my skills." "I *will* figure out why I'm not happy in my job." "I *will* look for a new opportunity."

Don't these statements make you feel stronger? It's almost like a law of physics: if you want new results, you have to do something different. Change is nothing more than doing something differently.

4. Make a definitive commitment to yourself.

Once you've made change a *will*, you can take the fourth and final step in implementing change into your life: you can make a definitive commitment to yourself. You can expand upon the "I will change," to include "when" and "why."

On the next blank, right-hand page in your notebook write, "Why Will I Change?" Answer this question in as much detail as possible. After you have answered it, on the next blank, right-hand page in your notebook write at the top, "When Will I Change?" and write your answer. (You may use pages 103-104 for these two questions.)

By answering these questions, you are making a commitment to allow change to happen. You are programming your subconscious to follow the direction *you* want to go. Read your responses to these two questions often, because your answers will keep you on course.

As someone who has made a commitment to overcome the fear of change, you can make change work on your behalf. Because this is so important, let's review the four simple strategies:

1. Make your internal mechanism look at change positively. Trade the word "change" for the word "adventure."

2. Ask yourself how change will benefit you. Write out positive questions and carry them with you. Look at them often, especially in times of doubt.

3. Know that change is a *will*, not a *should*.

4. Confirm the commitment to yourself by answering the questions "When and why will I change?"

By ridding yourself of the fear of change, you will regain control of your thinking and your beliefs. Once you have control, all you'll need are strategies for putting your plan into action.

WHY WILL I CHANGE?

_____

_____

_____

_____

_____

_____

_____

_____

_____

_____

_____

_____

_____

_____

_____

_____

_____

_____

_____

_____

_____

_____

_____

_____

_____

WHEN WILL I CHANGE?

8

Achieving What You Want

lmost fifty percent of the work force suffers from physical or emotional symptoms of burnout. It is estimated that stress costs companies $7,500 per employee annually in lost productivity and absenteeism. In recent years, stress in the work place has risen twenty-five to thirty percent. The mental stress caused by a lack of job security, greater work loads, stalled careers, and working in the wrong job, takes a large toll on peoples' health. High blood pressure, skin maladies, headaches, back pain, and even cancer, are all accelerated by stress. Your job is life threatening if:

❑ You never have enough time.

❑ You're always tense at work.

❑ You're too busy to eat properly.

❑ You feel you're under constant pressure.

105

- ❑ You feel guilty about the time you spend working.
- ❑ You cancel personal appointments to make more time for work.
- ❑ At the end of your work day you have no energy for personal activities or relationships.

What do you suppose is the leading cause of heart attacks in the United States? A recent study by the National Institute of Health revealed that the leading cause of heart attacks is the happiness factor: how happy people are with their lives. The number two cause, which is very closely linked with the happiness factor, is: job satisfaction.

When you work at a job you enjoy and when you use your natural talents and skills, you have a more balanced life, which has a positive effect on your body. Your immune system runs at top speed and your overall health is greatly enhanced. When you enjoy yourself, you naturally laugh and smile more. Healing messages flow through your body. And, when you do what you're meant to do, your work performance excels, and the world in general benefits from your uniqueness.

We've already discussed the fact that most people have randomly selected their careers; they did not choose a career based upon their talents. This approach was okay in the past, when people were pretty much guaranteed long-term employment, but it is not viable today. What is important today is that you do what comes naturally; only then can you enjoy job security and job satisfaction.

In a recent survey, retirees were asked "What do you regret most about your life?" Out of all the possible answers, the second biggest regret they shared was staying in the wrong career or job. *You* don't have to end up this way upon your retirement. Whether you are just starting your career—or if you are in the middle of it—you can take control of your future **now**. You can find the job best-suited to your talents and skills.

Daily Activity Analysis

To assure that your actions lead you to your goal, there is another exercise for you to complete. You will need to keep a **Daily Activity Log** for a minimum of one week. The purpose of this log is to track how and where you spend your time.

About a year ago I first met Elizabeth, a vibrant woman in her fifties. Elizabeth was very action-oriented. She worked full-time as a college professor and a student counselor, and she was very active in community affairs. To keep up with her responsibilities, Elizabeth worked fifteen-hour days. Yet she always felt guilty about never having enough time to accomplish her personal goals. (Elizabeth had a deep yearning to write a book. In fact, she had agreed to co-write a book with an associate; however, she had not written even one word.) This anxiety was causing her a great deal of stress.

To determine how and where Elizabeth spent her fifteen hours, I instructed her to keep a Daily Activity Log for one week. After tracking her activities for the week, she was able to analyze what she did with her time. Elizabeth finally understood the cause of her stress and unhappiness: she was spending far too much time on things which were not important to her.

So, Elizabeth made the decision to spend less time on less important activities, thereby making room for what she wanted to do, like writing the book. By streamlining the preparations for her classes, and by letting other people take over some of her community activities, Elizabeth found she had "free" time each day! Not only was she able to use these hours to write, she actually felt she accomplished more in less time.

By keeping a log of her activities, Elizabeth was able to

prioritize her schedule, which gave her a renewed sense of accomplishment. Her self-induced stress decreased dramatically.

You can do the same. It is amazingly simple. In your notebook—or use a separate notebook specifically for your Daily Activity Log—monitor how you spend your time each day, for at least one week. After the week has ended, review your activities and the amount of time you spent on each. Judge each activity based on its contribution to what you want to do—your mission in life. Highlight each activity which prevents you from moving towards your goal; the clutter in your life.

After reviewing your Daily Activity Log, you will be able to better prioritize your days. Determine the importance of each unhighlighted activity (your priorities). Take action on your number one priority until it is accomplished, and then move on to the next priority. By eliminating the clutter in your life, you will be amazed at the extra hours you have created, and the amount of work you will accomplish once you have refocused your energy.

Determining Your Situation

Everyone's situation is unique, and there are many variables which must be considered before you take action. Remember the job success formula: If you are using the talents and skills you enjoy, if your values are being met, and you feel as though you are making a difference; you will love your job.

If you've just graduated from school or you're currently unemployed, you'll need to persuade someone that you can add value or solve a problem for them.

If you are employed and established in a career, you must decide if you love what you do. Do you mostly enjoy your job, or not? Are there things you could change about your current job to bring it in line with your talents and values? Are the parts of your job you dislike essential to your job? How do the parts of your job you enjoy compare with your strengths? If you feel your job is worth some changes, go for it. Maybe you'll decide to stay in the same field, but change employers, or maybe you'll decide to change careers entirely.

And, you could possibly find yourself in a situation that hasn't yet been discussed. Maybe you currently earn a good salary, which supports a very comfortable life-style for you and your family. You are successful, yet you're bored and dissatisfied with your work. Each day is another drudgery. You can't imagine doing the same thing for another ten or twenty years, but you don't want to jeopardize your family's life-style. What can you do?

Several months back I had lunch with a successful dentist, who was in his mid-thirties. "Tom," he said to me, "do you know what I'll be doing next Monday?"

"No," I answered, "what will you be doing?"

"Looking in someone's mouth. And, do you know what I'll be doing the following Monday, and next month, and next year? The same thing. Over and over again."

"Is there something else you'd rather be doing?" I questioned.

"I'm sure there is," he responded, "but I don't know what. Besides, I have a big house with a large mortgage, two kids in private school, and car payments. It would be traumatic to give any of that up. Yet, the thought of practicing dentistry for the next twenty-five years depresses me."

As we delved into his interests and compared them with some of his latent talents, a strong desire to speak professionally surfaced. The thought of speaking to groups of his peers excited him, I could see it in his eyes. Yet, he knew he couldn't afford to quit his practice to pursue this dream. So, he got creative. What if he began speaking on a part-time basis and still kept his practice? He could acquire some speaking experience, while testing the waters.

He did—and he loved it! He began to speak once a month, then once a week, until finally he began addressing dental conferences and conventions on a regular basis.

This new addition to his job, professional speaking, revitalized his life. He realized he didn't need to quit dentistry, because the reduction in office hours, which was required by his speaking engagements, was enough of a diversion to bring a positive feeling into his life. Additionally, his speaking fees made up for any lost income from his practice.

What a compromise. What a win-win strategy. He was so enthused about his new venture, both his work and home life were revitalized.

What about you? Can you begin working on a dream, on a part-time basis? You don't always have to give-up everything you've worked for to follow your passion. You can enter the road to revitalization slowly, and still be amazed at the difference it can make in your life.

Think outside the box. Think creatively. Brainstorm with family and friends. Remember what Dr. Dentist did for his life.

Seven Keys to Taking Action and Creating Change

You've set your goal and you are determined to stop wasting time on activities which prevent you from working towards it. Unfortunately, even with the best plan, self doubt and other obstacles are apt to interfere with your progress. To keep yourself on course, below are seven things you can do to achieve the changes you want.

⨯ Key #1 ⨯
Give yourself permission to use your unique talents and skills in ways which meet your interests and values.

It is okay to pursue your mission, to do whatever it is you want to do. The only person you need approval from is yourself.

I'm certain you've met people who seem inspired. Their enthusiasm is evident in everything they do. They seem to have found true happiness; you know they aren't faking it. It is a pretty good bet that their life work is in line with what they were *meant* to do. People who have a clear focus enjoy greater job satisfaction and life fulfillment.

I once worked with a gentleman who had eight years of experience in human resources. His job was being phased out, and he needed to figure out what to do next in his life. "What would you like to do?" I asked him.

"Well, human resources, I guess. That's where my experience is."

"You don't sound too sure," I replied.

"Well, I really don't like it that much," he explained. "but it's what I've done for eight years."

"Do you want to continue doing something you don't like very much for the next forty years?"

"Not really," he said. "But what else can I do?"

Because he didn't know his talents and values, nor where he might be of service or make a contribution, he feared change. Once I guided him through career analysis, he discovered things about himself he had never known. It turned out he had a natural interest in marketing and research. He ended up staying with the same company, but in the marketing and research department. Because of his new-found direction, his career and life were both reenergized. No longer was his life based on ifs and fears. He gave himself permission to investigate *who* he was and to discover *what* he could do.

⋆ Key #2 ⋆
Throw away your excuses and begin to view life through changed and renewed beliefs about yourself and your abilities.

What prevents you from doing what you want? What is your excuse? Who do you want in charge of your life? Will you create the life you want by using the unique skills and talents you enjoy using—or will someone else dictate how you live?

I recently counseled a woman who had worked as a nurse for twenty years. By the time we met, she had been promoted to a high administrative position in a hospital. One day, out of the blue, she was told the hospital no longer required her services. At first, she was shocked and angry. However, as she talked about her situation and discussed her interests, she realized she hadn't been happy doing what she did. "I'm tired of just making money for a hospital," she said. "I want to start helping people again. I think I'd like to go to Mexico, learn Spanish, and work with the poor—or maybe I could move out West and work in a small clinic for American Indians."

After a couple of weeks of deep soul searching and creative thinking about her career and her life, she returned to my office. She looked like a different person. Her face was bright. She appeared upbeat and very relaxed. "I need to tell you something I didn't mention before," she said. "When I was growing up, I always wanted to go into interior decorating, but my father said, 'Daughter, nursing is for you. It's very professional and you'll never have trouble finding a job. Maybe you'll even marry a doctor someday.' So, I went into nursing, and I've been a nurse for twenty years. I never even *wanted* to be a nurse! Well, I called my father last night and told him how I felt about nursing. He broke down and cried. But, do you know what came of our discussion? I am now going to school for interior decorating! I'll do some nursing while I'm in school, to pay the bills, but when I finish, I'll get into interior decorating. I'm so excited! I can't wait to get started."

At that moment, she had begun to view her life differently. She had a renewed belief about herself and her abilities. She had gained control of her life and she was committed to her mission. After twenty years, she had finally let go of her excuse. Are you ready to leave your excuses behind?

↜ Key #3 ↝
Believe in yourself.

You now understand your talents and skills, and you know how to cross-transfer them into whatever it is you want to do. You know your values and how they guide your life. Now you must trust your abilities.

Use the techniques we discussed to create a winning belief system and how to overcome fear to create internal confidence. Reward yourself for small accomplishments along the way of your journey to success and happiness. The empowering belief in **you** will grow stronger and stronger.

When a young boy asked Walt Disney what the key was to his success, Mr. Disney responded it was "belief." Remember the survey of successful sales people? They also attributed their success to "belief." When you have confidence in yourself, it will be much easier for you to take action.

A few years ago, I coached Bill, who had been laid off by the company he had worked at for twelve years. He experienced the typical emotions of shock, anger, and fear. But, when he got over those feelings and took control of his life, he started a video production business.

Nine months later, I visited Bill at his home. This was the first time I had met his wife, and she shared a story with me. She said, "When Bill was working at the company, he often had dreams of starting his own business, but I never let him. I'd say, 'Bill, we have a mortgage. We have two kids. The company pays you every week and they provide benefits. You can't leave that.'

"When Bill was laid off and we *had* to do something, it gave him the opportunity to start his business. It hasn't been easy. As with most new businesses, we've had our ups and downs; but, I'll tell you this: I have never seen Bill happier in his life than during these past nine months. I have never seen him so determined, nor have I seen him accomplish so much. I wish I had let Bill do this years ago."

Not only did Bill believe in his capabilities, he was excited by what he was doing. And his family was enjoying a happier Bill!

To reach the point of believing in yourself and of taking action to move you in the direction of your goal, all you have to do is Key #4.

⁘ Key #4 ⁘
Make a decision to do it.

This sounds so simple, but sometimes it is the hardest step to take. Think about it. If you have a goal to do something, it will stay a dream until you take action to make it a reality. *Thinking* about a change in your life or *thinking* about a new job or career will not *make* it happen. Taking action will.

Have a clear objective. Know how and where you want to use your talents and skills. Your brain functions on clarity. When you send specific signals on a continuous basis, your subconscious becomes conditioned to automatically move you in the direction of the signals. A decision is difficult to come by when you are unsure about what to do. That's when you do nothing. You procrastinate because your brain is not getting clear signals.

Think about a traffic light. When it is red, it is a clear signal to stop. When it is green, it is a clear signal to go. On the other hand, yellow is kind of iffy. What if traffic lights only blinked yellow? There would be mass confusion and gridlock. Nothing would move. That's exactly what happens when your brain doesn't receive a clear signal: gridlock.

You now have the tools to evaluate your talents and to determine what you are meant to do in your career—and your life. Use these tools. Give your brain the clear signal it needs and it will be easy for you to begin acting on your desires.

Use whatever it is in your job or career which is bothering you the most as your incentive. Whether you are stressed out, unhappy, bored, have a lousy boss, or you are not using your skills, you can decide to do something about it right now. Go ahead, decide! That didn't take long, did it? Don't you feel better, now that you're ready to pursue your goal?

Good. Keep feeding the fire of desire. It's too easy to lose focus and to get off track. How many times have you heard an uplifting presentation that inspired you to do some things differently? But as soon as you turned off the tape or walked out of the presentation, your determination waned, and you never got around to making any changes.

The actions which you've taken so far in this book are too important to the rest of your life for you to allow the flame to die. The way to keep your fire burning is to feel so strongly about your reasons for wanting to change your job or career, that your conviction to make it happen intensifies every day. In your mind you need to associate emotions of happiness, contentment, satisfaction, and excitement with the changes you are about to make; while associating emotions of unhappiness, discontent, and dissatisfaction with your present situation. To help you keep the fire roaring, follow Key #5.

↜ Key #5 ↝
List all of the reasons why you are unhappy in your present job or career.

You can make your list on page 118 or in your career notebook on the next blank, right-hand page write, "Reasons Why I Am Unhappy." Make your list as long as you can, and be specific. Give this list some thought, as it is very important for your motivation. Go ahead. Write down why you are disenchanted with your current situation.

The next step is for you to determine why a change in each situation would make you happier. How would your level or quality of work change? How would your opinion of the organization or industry change? For example, let's say the first reason you listed is that you are unhappy because your supervisor is always looking over your shoulder. On the first line under, "Why A Change Would Make Me Happier," you might comment, that if given more freedom, you would be far less stressed. With more freedom to work on your own, you would be more creative, thereby producing better results. Additionally, you would be excited to go to work, rather than dreading each work day.

Follow this line of thinking for each of the reasons you have given for your unhappiness. You may write your correspondent responses on page 120 or in your career notebook, at the top of the next blank, right-hand page write, "Why A Change Would Make Me Happier."

Do not give up. If you haven't finished your list, stop reading and return to the above exercise. It is that important. This is a project on your life.

Once you have listed your reasons and your explanations, the decision to change your life will be much clearer. The extraordinary gains which you perceive will overpower any fear and doubt you might have about initiating change. When your brain perceives personal gain and pleasant emotions, your subconscious will drive you to action, and your enthusiasm to continue remains strong. This will keep your fire burning.

↲ Key #6 ↳
Learn from yourself.

Another technique to overcome procrastination is to learn from your past actions. During your life, you've made decisions—and you've made changes. What made you decide? What made you change? Was it because if you didn't do it, something bad would have happened or did you do it because it made you happier, or you could earn more money, or was it better for your family? What was your thought process? What was your motivation? Once you remember what drove you to do things in the past, you can use the same procedure to get yourself to do something now.

For example, my son always works best when he has an impending deadline. So, whenever he must accomplish something, he sets his own deadline, and this moves him to action.

Think about your personal motivational formula—and use it to make things happen.

↲ Key #7 ↳
Be persistent.

Stay with it. If things don't happen overnight, don't give up. Take the action you believe will produce the results you want. Analyze your results. If they are not exactly what you were after, simply change your action and achieve new results.

People who are successful have had many more results in their lives because they stayed at it: they were persistent. Babe Ruth struck out 1,330 times; but what do we remember? His home run record. Which pitcher holds the record for throwing the most wild pitches? It's the same pitcher who holds the record for the most strike outs: Nolan Ryan.

There are thousands of other examples (you may know some yourself). No matter who, the tools for success remain the same:

1. Give yourself permission to use your unique talents in ways which meet your interests.

REASONS WHY I AM UNHAPPY

1. _____
2. _____
3. _____
4. _____
5. _____
6. _____
7. _____
8. _____
9. _____
10. _____
11. _____
12. _____
13. _____
14. _____
15. _____
16. _____
17. _____
18. _____

2. Get rid of your excuses.

3. Believe in yourself.

4. Make a decision to get it done.

5. List your reasons for being unhappy and why a change will help.

6. Learn from your past actions.

7. Be persistent.

Understand that the actions you take are creating a future that you want; not a future you just floated into nor one which someone pulled you into. This future is of your design. And when you design it, you own it. Life will mean so much more to you.

I have given you a success formula, a process to follow which will help you discover and fulfill your mission in life. You know who you are and what you can do. You know that a richer, more satisfying life is yours for the taking.

The next phase of your career cure is to locate the opportunity which fulfills your mission. After analyzing yourself and your career, maybe you've decided to start your own business, to be an entrepreneur. If this is the case, you should read Chapter Fourteen, as it will confirm whether or not self-employment is agreeable to your personality and skills. (The information in Part Three and Part Four can be of great value to you when you look for people to hire.)

If you are following the more traditional path—that of being an employee—how can you persuade or convince someone that, in fact, *you* can add value or solve a problem for them? The powerful job search strategies in Part Three are different than the ones you've heard or read about before. This is good, because you will stand above the crowd and get the job, despite all of the competition. These strategies work, they're easy to use, and they make the job search fun!

So, go ahead. Get excited as you continue your revitalization. In the next chapter, I'll discuss some of the things you might have done in the past, but won't be doing in the future: the nineteen deadly sins of job searching.

Why A Change Would Make Me Happier

1. _____

2. _____

3. _____

4. _____

5. _____

6. _____

7. _____

8. _____

9. _____

10. _____

11. _____

12. _____

13. _____

14. _____

15. _____

16. _____

17. _____

18. _____

Part Three

Succeeding
In Your Job Search

Avoiding The 19 Job Search Sins

During your pursuit of a new job, you will have serious competition. There are *a lot* of people looking for a new occupa-
tion. However, by following the advice in this book, you will
stand out from your competition. And, by reading this chapter, you will
learn exactly what to do—and what not to do—as you search for your
career opportunity.

The art of finding a job has many components. Like a smooth-running engine, each component must be working properly and in tune
with the others. Each part of your job search must be done well or your
efforts could fail. Just one mistake can negate all of the things you did
correctly—and you won't receive the job offer you want.

Relatively few people have the knowledge you will have after reading
this book. The lucky few who have been trained in these techniques

enter the job market with confidence; they successfully locate new jobs and careers in line with their desires. You will do the same.

In life, we usually learn more from our mistakes—and undesired results—than we do from our successes; so, a good place for us to start is by examining nineteen job search sins you must avoid.

❧ Sin #1 ☙
Not knowing your qualifications.

The job search is very much a marketing and sales endeavor. *You* are the product and you must convince others that *they* need you. If you don't know your qualifications (skills and talents), if you don't know how you can benefit someone, if you can't state what you've done in the past—or what your potential is—you cannot effectively sell yourself.

Most people are unable to intelligently discuss their talents and skills, much less how they can benefit a company. So, before starting your job search, make sure you know and understand who you are, what you can do, and what you prefer to do.

❧ Sin #2 ☙
Having a bad attitude.

Interviewers pick up clues from your facial and body gestures, and by the words you use. If you have a sour or pessimistic outlook on life, these feelings will become known during the interview. Additionally, if you have a negative attitude, you probably appear as though you lack self-confidence. Most employers will not hire a dark cloud—a positive attitude opens the door to opportunity.

One of the traits successful people share is that they surround themselves with people who are upbeat and positive. They know that the quickest and surest way to drag themselves down is to listen to a negative thinker.

↜ Sin #3 ↝
Not being committed to your job search.

Finding a job opportunity requires a considerable amount of time and energy. When done correctly, looking for an employment opportunity is a full-time job. People who treat their job search as a part-time endeavor usually accept a position that turns out to be just another job, which soon leads to work disenchantment.

It is vital to complete the career assessment exercises in Part One and Part Two prior to the start of your job search. Before you are able to design your future, you need to determine what is best for you. Once you've done that properly, a strong commitment on your part has already been made. If you don't have a strong will to make it happen, you will find the search too difficult, become frustrated, and either quit the search or accept a mediocre assignment. You need the right goal and the right attitude to make the commitment.

↜ Sin #4 ↝
Keeping your job search a secret.

To find the best job opportunity, you must seek out the opinion of as many people as possible. Remember, this is a marketing effort and the more people you tell about your product, the more chances you have of selling it. The old notion of being ashamed because you were looking for a job is outdated. You should not keep your search a secret. You will find that people are your greatest resource during a job search.

↜ Sin #5 ↝
Setting out to fill an opening rather than trying to provide a service.

Too many people ask potential employers, "Do you have any openings?" It doesn't matter. What you need to do is show a potential employer that they will benefit by hiring you. Good employees are always in demand. If you can demonstrate how your skills can solve a problem and add value to the company, or how you can do something better than someone who's doing it now, or how you can do something that no one else in the company is able to do, you will receive an offer—even if a position wasn't open.

I'm often asked, "How is the job market in Florida or Arizona or California?" My response is usually the same, "The market has needs. What you must do is find the hidden job market. It's about more than just openings." (See Chapter 11.)

❧ Sin #6 ❧
Depending on your resume, an employment agency, or a recruiter to find you a job.

Many people mistakenly believe that having a good resume guarantees they will receive a good job offer. Although a well-prepared resume is essential, it is only *one* tool, and it should not be relied upon to get you a good offer.

Furthermore, only ten percent of the work force finds a job through an employment agency or a recruiter. Relying solely on these third parties and making no other efforts on your behalf will prolong your search. You will probably not find an opportunity that matches your skills and values.

❧ Sin #7 ❧
Using classified ads as your sole source.

Reading help wanted ads is the most-often used method of looking for a job. Since so many people use this method, you will have tremendous competition (which lessens your chance of success). Like employment agencies and recruiters, reading classifieds should be a part of your job search, but not the only thing you do.

Did you know that only thirty percent of all available positions are ever advertised in the classifieds? That means, if you only answered the classifieds, you would miss out on *seventy percent* of the job opportunities! (When you do answer a classified ad, there is an approach you can follow which will set you apart from the competition. See Chapter 11.)

⚮ Sin #8 ⚮
Not answering your telephone.

When you fill out employment applications and send out your resume, your telephone number should be a part of the information you provide to the potential employer. Although you are not expected to sit by your telephone waiting for it to ring, an answering machine or voice mail service should take incoming messages whenever you are not available to answer the phone.

Imagine a manager leafing through a stack of resumes. After reading your resume, they want to talk with you. They telephone your number, but the phone just rings. No person or machine answers their call. Where do you think the manager will put your resume? Off to the side for another try later—or to the bottom of the stack? Why take the chance? Make sure that someone or something answers your phone.

⚮ Sin #9 ⚮
Talking only with people who work in personnel or human resources.

It is wrong to assume that only the people who work in these departments have the authority to hire people. Yes, in larger companies they administer personnel matters (like the hiring process), but they aren't usually the ones who decide who is or isn't hired. That decision typically falls on the manager or supervisor of a specific department: the hiring authority.

⋊ Sin #10 ⋉
"Winging it" at interviews.

An interview is an opportunity to be your best. It is your chance to show the hiring authority what you have that the other job candidates don't. If you haven't done any research on the company and if you haven't decided why you're interested in joining the company, you'll come across as uninterested and unenthusiastic during the interview.

The better prepared you are and the more you know about the company, the greater your chances are of receiving an offer. By practicing answers to typical interview questions (see pages 176 and 187), and by having a plan of action to sell yourself as the best possible candidate for the job, the more relaxed and confident you will be. All of these factors add up to: success.

⋊ Sin #11 ⋉
Exhibiting bad manners.

Arriving too early or too late for an interview, being rude on the telephone, using offensive language, not paying attention to your grooming or how you dress, and bringing someone (friend, spouse, child, etc.) with you to the interview will be frowned upon and could have a very negative effect on the hiring decision. Good planning on your part can avoid most of these difficulties. Make sure you know how long it will take you to travel to the interview, i.e., what traffic conditions you should expect. Again, when you go to an interview, employers assume you are presenting your best; anything less than that will hurt you.

⋊ Sin #12 ⋉
Being dishonest.

Nine times out of ten, anything you say which is less than the truth will come back to haunt you. This includes little white lies, hiding information, fabricating information, and telling the hiring authority what *you* think *they* want to hear.

Additionally, if you feel the need to provide false information to make yourself look more attractive to the interviewer, the job probably isn't the right one for you. Realize, there are two purposes for an interview: to sell yourself and to determine if the company, the management, and the skills required for the position are in line with your goals. To have a successful interview, you must be completely honest with the interviewer and make sure they are being completely honest with you.

❧ Sin #13 ❧
A failure to develop rapport.

As you talk with people on the phone and as you meet people personally, particularly at the interview stage, developing rapport is a must. Rapport is developed when another person believes that you are like them. (Fifty-five to sixty-five percent of rapport building is through body language: kinesthetics.) Maybe the two of you have things in common: you talk in a similar fashion, you have common mannerisms, or you have common interests. All of these similarities contribute to building rapport. Without rapport, you probably won't receive a job offer.

You must try to build rapport with everyone, including the security guard, the receptionist, the secretary, the hiring manager—and anyone else in between. You never know who might have input in the final hiring decision. If you're able to develop rapport with someone, you are eighty percent of the way to a job offer! That's right. Eighty percent of the decisions to hire a person are based on personality, not on qualifications.

❧ Sin #14 ❧
Inquiring about salary and benefits
at the beginning of the interview.

Asking about salary and other compensation early in the interview shows too much of a ME-orientation. Remember, your main mission during an interview is to sell yourself, to let the hiring authority know what *you* can do for *them*. You must convince the company that you are the right person for the position. Get them interested in you, and the topic of compensation will occur naturally during the interview.

Additionally, the more the interviewer feels they need you, the more they are willing to offer you. At the beginning of the interview, the interviewer doesn't even know *if* they need you—you haven't had time to sell yourself. During the course of the interview, your worth as an employee becomes more evident.

∿ Sin #15 ∾
Not asking questions at the interview.

Many people erroneously believe that their responsibility during an interview is only to answer the questions asked of them. If all hiring authorities were highly skilled interviewers, this might be true. Unfortunately, very few managers and supervisors have this skill, which means you must be prepared to take control of the interview.

First, you must get your sales points across. The interviewer must know why the company would benefit from hiring you. By asking the right questions, you can demonstrate these benefits. For example, you could ask questions like: "Would it help your business to have someone who is bilingual?" "Does the candidate for this job need good people skills?" "Would the fact that I was trained in computer spread sheets be of help to you?"

Second, hiring managers look for enthusiasm in a candidate. The right questions show enthusiasm.

And third, in order for you to evaluate the company (before accepting an offer), you will have to ask questions.

∿ Sin #16 ∾
Talking negatively about previous employers and bosses.

Most people don't realize the harm this type of conversation can cause. If you make derogatory comments about past employers and past supervisors, the interviewer will have concerns about hiring you. Their thought is that someday you might feel the same about their company, and they don't want negative publicity.

Keep your comments positive, or at least turn negatives into positives. Be careful when you are asked questions like: "Tell me about the worst boss you ever had." "What were some of the things about your last employer that bothered you the most?" (I'll give specifics on how to handle this type of questioning in Chapter 12.)

❧ Sin #17 ❧
Keeping your accomplishments to yourself.

The job search process is a marketing endeavor. You must talk about the benefits of your product—you—which are demonstrated by your accomplishments.

Based on what you've accomplished in the past, the interviewer will make assumptions about what you can do for them. If you don't talk about your accomplishments, they cannot evaluate you properly. Additionally, your accomplishments give credibility to the talents and skills you claim to possess.

❧ Sin #18 ❧
Emphasizing your weaknesses and criticizing yourself.

No one is perfect; we all have faults. However, my advice to you is: never leave a dangling negative. If you are asked about a weakness, follow it up with a positive.

Here's an example: Let's say you stated that two years ago, during a performance review at your last job, you rated low in organizational skills. Determined to improve your rating, you talked to people who were very good at organization and asked them for their advice on how to improve your organization skills. You also attended a training conference on organizational strategies. At your last performance review, one year ago, you received a nine out of ten rating on organization!

What you've done is turned a negative into a positive. You did not leave a dangling negative: "I was once told I had poor organizational skills."

Remember, you are at the interview to show the best you can be.

⊱ Sin #19 ⊰
Not asking for the job.

There are many things in life you could have, if only you asked. The same holds true in the working world. How many interviews end with the interviewer saying, "Do you have any further questions?"

And you respond, "No. I think you've answered all of my questions."

"Well, thanks so much for coming in," concludes the interviewer. "We'll try to get back to you in a couple of weeks."

Would a good sales person end an interview this way? When the interviewer asked if there were any further questions, a good sales person would have said, "Yes, just one."

"Well, what is it?" responds the interviewer.

"You know, Mr. Interviewer," says the salesperson, "we had a very good visit today. I understand what you need and I'm confident my skills and talents can make a great contribution to helping your company meet its goals. I'm very enthused about the opportunity and I'm anxious to get started. When can I begin?" That's how a good salesperson would close the sale.

Oftentimes, this type of a close will result in an offer. But, even if it doesn't, because other candidates are yet to be interviewed, or whatever, you have demonstrated genuine enthusiasm for the job, and that can be very much in your favor.

That's it. Nineteen job search sins for you to avoid. Refer to this list often, especially prior to an interview. If you avoid these major faux pas, have a well-designed resume which includes the appropriate information, and know how to use your resume—then you'll stay well ahead of your competition.

10

The Realities Of Resumes

I will begin my discussion on resumes by being brutally honest. I don't like them. I dislike resumes for three reasons: they are used to screen *out* applicants, the reading of resumes is a very *subjective* process, and when you send out a resume you can *lose control* of your job search.

When hiring authorities flip through a stack of resumes, they are determining which resumes can be discarded or set aside. They will look at a resume until they see something negative, at which point they will throw it away; no longer must they deal with that piece of paper again. I truly believe that, subconsciously or not, when sitting in front of a pile of resumes, the first goal of hiring authorities is to see how quickly then can make the stack shrink.

Secondly, you do not know what a particular person will consider negative. Each person has their own biases, and different people will read the *same* resume differently. You never know what information on your resume might be the cause of your resume being tossed, which is why you should never include the following information on a resume. It can quickly be used against you in the selection process.

- ❑ Date of Birth
- ❑ Marital Status
- ❑ Number of Dependents
- ❑ A Photograph of Yourself
- ❑ Health Statistics, including your height and weight
- ❑ Religious or Political Affiliations
- ❑ Social Security Number
- ❑ Expected Salary
- ❑ Race or National Origin

Thirdly, after you mail out your resume you must wait and hope for a response. You have lost control of the process, which is not a position you want to be in when it involves your life.

Fact: submitting your resume is one of the least effective means of job hunting.

The Resume

With that said, it is true that a first-rate resume is a necessary *tool* in the job search process. From years of experience, I know what works and what doesn't work, what you should include and what you should exclude from your resume.

The purpose of a resume is to produce an interview (that is where you can receive a job offer). Think of your resume as an ad for a product. The product being you—your skills and abilities as an employee. Anyone who reads your ad (resume) is a potential employer. However, if they don't read the ad, they won't buy the product. To assure that your resume is read, you must avoid the following problems:

1. Too Long.

Once I received a twenty-six page resume. No, I did not read it. Keep yours brief; no longer than two pages.

2. Listing only duties and responsibilities.

Management wants to know about *you*. What drives you? What values will you bring to the company? How would they benefit by hiring you? State your accomplishments, not just a list of responsibilities.

3. Extensive data on what you did years ago.

Managers are most interested in what you've done during the last five years. The further back in time you go, the less detail you should provide.

4. Disorganized format.

A lack of organization and an inconsistent format will not portray the image you want to present. Your resume should be easy to read and the data should be well organized.

5. Grammatical errors.

Any spelling errors within the resume can cause your demise. Be careful with the terminology you use. Sometimes what you write is not what you mean. Here are a couple of examples of how the written word can be misconstrued:

> This afternoon there will be a meeting in the south and north end of the church. Children will be baptized at both ends.
> Thursday at 5:00 p.m. there will be a meeting of the Little Mother's Club. All those wishing to become little mothers, please meet the pastor in his study.

6. Messy copies.

What image are you trying to present? Crinkly or torn paper with smudges and white-out is not acceptable. It is best to have your resume printed on a laser printer or professionally produced.

7. Getting too cute with the presentation.

Some people believe if they print their resume on bright, loud-colored paper, it will be singled out from the competition. Or if they use a bold, dramatic format to get their message across (like cartoons and graphics), their resume will be remembered. Most managers do *not* look favorably upon unusual styles of resumes.

Although I encourage individuality and creativity, the resume is a rather conservative document. Usually it is best if you keep yours conservative. My suggestion is to use a white or off-white paper stock (either laid or linen), with dark ink.

Yes, there are times when this rule can be broken, particularly if you are looking for a creative position. For example: John, a recent college graduate with a degree in marketing, sent hundreds of "traditional" resumes all over the country, with very little success. He decided to change his approach, by designing a unique package for his resume: John had a picture of himself when he was five years old printed on the side of a milk carton, along with some clever copy. He enclosed his resume inside the carton, which was then sealed.

He received far more attention the second time around, and his creativity paid off. Realize, this approach worked because John was seeking an opportunity to utilize his creativity. If he had been looking for a job at a bank, the milk carton probably wouldn't have made it out of the mail room.

Use discretion. If you're unsure, follow a conservative design.

Resume Format

Remember, the sole purpose of a resume is to open the door for an interview. Therefore, your document must be better prepared than those of your competition. As you design the format of your resume, there are some things you should take into consideration:

❑ A resume should not be longer than two pages.

❑ Keep it concise, logical, and accomplishment-oriented.

❑ Always be honest and factual; yet don't volunteer information in the resume which might preclude an interview.

❑ Design the layout so the resume is easy to read. Allow for white space between categories. Underline, capitalize, or use bold-faced type for headlines and major items.

❑ Check your spelling and grammar. Have someone proofread the resume. A misspelled word can cost you an interview.

❑ Type the resume neatly. In today's word processing age, there should be absolutely no erasures, smudges or white-outs on your document. It should be reproduced cleanly, or better yet, printed on a laser printer.

❑ Generally speaking, stay away from offbeat or cute formats.

> An employer spends an average of ten
> seconds reading your resume.

There are basically two ways to organize the data on your resume: chronologically or functionally. A chronological format lists your work and education in reverse chronological order, with your most recent experience listed first. The functional format has specific skill areas and breaks out your experience relative to each skill.

There are advantages to both formats, depending on your situation. Based on my experience in hiring practices, I believe most managers prefer a chronological format, because they find it easier to follow. However, my preference is somewhat of a combination. A dynamic summary of your qualifications listed near the top of the resume is effective. Also, a section titled, "Skills and Traits," where you list the skills you enjoy using and the character traits you possess (which you think might be used in the position you're seeking) can be beneficial.

Underneath each employer you list on your resume, I suggest a couple of brief sentences which give an overview of your duties and responsibilities. Follow this information with a few of your accomplishments, listed in a bullet-format, so that they stand out. The accomplishments you include should be the best of those you identified in Part One. They should demonstrate your most desirable traits and the skills you enjoy using most.

Those are my ideas. Should you use a chronological or functional format? Ultimately, the choice is yours. Your best bet is to take all of the concepts presented in this chapter, analyze them, and put together the resume which best represents you.

Resume Content

At the top center of the page, put your full name (not a nickname), address (including city, state, and zip code), and telephone number.

Job Objective

The objective is optional. If you choose to include a job objective, you should use self-descriptive terminology, and indicate what you can do for a company. The objective should be specific enough to describe your field of interest, yet broad enough so as not to be overly limiting. Never over generalize, i.e., "I want to work with people." Let the hiring authority know what you can do for them.

Education

If your education is relevant and important for the position you are seeking, list it at the beginning of your resume. If you don't have the education that most people believe is required for a particular job, or education is not important for the position, you can put it at the end of your resume—or leave it off entirely.

If you are a college graduate, include the name and location of the college (and graduate school) from which you earned your degree, and the year the degree was awarded. Mention your major, minor(s), and any academic awards or honors you received. If your grade point average is 3.0 or greater (out of 4.0), list it.

Work Experience

This is the heart of the resume, so you should indicate the results you produced. Your work experience should be listed in reverse chronological order, with your most recent (or current) position stated first. Provide the name and location (city) of the employer, dates of employment, and job title(s) you held.

Unless a job title is self-explanatory, you should briefly describe your duties. Focus on the results you produced rather than the activities you performed. If you can quantify your accomplishments, do so. For instance, maybe you increased production by twenty-five percent or decreased costs by fifteen percent. Be selective. Choose your top three or four accomplishments and describe them, using action-oriented words (see page 142).

Additional Information

This is an optional section intended to cover items which don't logically fit under the other headings. Examples include: fluency in foreign languages, special certifications, licenses, or other skills and abilities.

Personal Interests

Make sure to stress hobbies, sports, and special interests which are related to your job objective. For example, if you are applying for a job as a communications engineer, you could list that you are a ham radio operator. You could also mention professional associations, fraternities, sororities, and other organizations to which you belong, if they are relevant to your career.

References

All that is needed is a statement that references are available upon request. If you are invited for an interview, be sure to bring the names, addresses, and phone numbers of your references with you. Also, you should contact each of your references beforehand, to obtain their permission to use them as a reference.

Cover Letters

When you forward a resume to a potential employer, you should also send a cover letter, which should be addressed to a specific individual within the company—or someone you have selected based on their authority to offer you a job.

Your cover letter should be short, to-the-point, and tailored for each prospective employer. The purpose of a cover letter is to tell that person how you can contribute to their operation.

Ideally, your cover letter is sent following a conversation with a hiring authority. The letter should address a particular point, don't repeat what is stated on your resume. Indicate how your interests and experience are applicable to this opportunity. Remember, your cover letter is another tool in marketing your background and skills. Ask yourself, what can I write that will make the reader want to interview me in person? You want to get face-to-face with this person, because a personal meeting is where opportunities are offered.

Cover Letter Format

Sometimes, a cover letter is more important than your resume. You need to communicate your enthusiasm and your desire to contribute to the company. You might mention specific characteristics of the firm which have impressed you or solutions to a problem you know the company has.

The appearance of your cover letter should be as professional as your resume, preferably on the same paper stock. Each cover letter should be typed and addressed accordingly. Always proofread your letter. Don't be screened out of the interview process because of a careless mistake.

A cover letter should consist of three paragraphs. In the first paragraph, introduce yourself and state how you heard about the company.

In paragraph two, explain why you are interested in the position, why you are qualified, and how you can contribute. Provide details of an achievement or an accomplishment which might impress the reader.

In the final paragraph, thank them for their time and indicate that you will telephone the hiring authority in one week to request an interview. Don't say, "I hope to hear from you soon." Waiting for them to contact you might take too long—allowing your competition the time to get in first. Telling the hiring authority that you will telephone them gives you control of the situation. You're not just waiting for the phone to ring. (You can even take this a step further by specifying on which day they can expect your call.)

The last paragraph can also be used to reaffirm your interest in the position (See Sample #1 Cover Letter on page 146).

The Reality

For every accepted job offer, over 1,450 resumes were sent out. That's right. One thousand four hundred and fifty resumes were mailed or faxed for every job offer that was accepted. If you don't mind those odds, go ahead, send your resume, and wait to see what happens.

However, by developing a personal marketing campaign, you can beat those odds and get the job offer.

KEY WORDS FOR RESUME PREPARATION

ACTION WORDS

Actively	Motivate
Accelerate	Organize
Adapt	Originate
Administer	Participate
Analyze	Perform
Approve	Plan
Coordinate	Pinpoint
Conceive	Program
Conduct	Propose
Complete	Prove
Control	Provide
Create	Proficient
Develop	Reduce
Demonstrate	Reinforce
Direct	Reorganize
Effect	Revamp
Eliminate	Responsible
Establish	Revise
Evaluate	Review
Expand	Schedule
Expedite	Significantly
Founded	Simplify
Generate	Set up
Increase	Solve
Influence	Strategy
Implement	Structure
Interpret	Streamline
Improve	Successfully
Lead	Supervise
Lecture	Support
Manage	Teach

SELF-DESCRIPTIVE WORDS

Active	Imaginative
Adaptive	Independent
Aggressive	Logical
Alert	Loyal
Ambitious	Mature
Analytical	Methodical
Aspiring	Objective
Attentive	Optimistic
Broad-minded	Perceptive
Conscientious	Perseverance
Consistent	Personable
Constructive	Pleasant
Creative	Positive
Dependable	Practical
Cheerful	Productive
Cooperative	Realistic
Diligent	Reliable
Determined	Resourceful
Diplomatic	Respective
Disciplined	Self-reliant
Discreet	Sense of Humor
Economical	Sincere
Efficient	Sophisticated
Energetic	Systematic
Enterprising	Tactful
Enthusiastic	Talented
Extroverted	Will Travel
Fair	Will Relocate
Forceful	

EDUCATIONAL WORDS

Academic	Knowledgeable
Determined	Learning Ability
Discipline	Scholarly
Graduate	Specialized

Source: Powell, C.R. *Career Planning and Placement Today*. Second Edition, Dubuque, Iowa: Kendall Hunt, 1978.

SAMPLE

William Graduate
87 N. Peck Avenue
LaGrange, Illinois 60525
(718) 000-1000

OBJECTIVE   Ambitious engineering graduate seeks to apply his education and experience to the growth and profitability of a progressive organization.

EDUCATION   University of Illinois
B.S. Electrical Engineering, June 1995 (3.8 gpa)

EXPERIENCE   **Engineering Department ~ University of Illinois**
1993-1995
Assisted undergraduate students in Engineering lab courses.
Organized exam correction methods for professors.
Lectured students on Power Technology.
Provided support to Engineering Administration.

Maximum Corporation, Hinsdale, Illinois
Summers 1991-1993
Engineering Intern
Assisted Project Engineers in design of high power systems.
Developed testing methods and introduced new products into production.
Improved manufacturing processes for existing product lines.
• Conceived new methods for product test resulting in $10,000 savings per quarter.
• Reduced manufacturing defects 10% by instituting new machine processes.

Yogurt Now, Ogden, Illinois
1989-1991 (part-time)
Assistant Manager
Prepared store for daily operation, served customers and trained new employees. Accounted for daily sales total and prepared Franchise Inventory Reports. Initiated and contributed to marketing procedures.
• Promoted to Assistant Manager after only 6 months of service (youngest to ever hold these responsibilities).
• Increased yogurt sales through off-site and coupon promotions.

ADDITIONAL
INFORMATION Fluent in German.

REFERENCES   Available on request.

SAMPLE

SUSAN JONES
1212 Career Lane
Ft. Lauderdale, Florida 33310
(305) 000-1000

SUMMARY

Financial professional with strong operational/ manufacturing expertise in small to medium-sized organizations. Diverse experience in consumer products, textiles, avionics, and electronics. Proven successes in start-up activities and turnaround situations. Developed and motivated staffs of thirty professionals.

* Effective Planner	* Results Oriented
* Team Player	* Problem Solver
* Responsible	* Enthusiastic

EDUCATION

B.S. Accounting, University of Florida, 1983.
C.P.A. Designation, 1985.

EXPERIENCE

McClain Components, Inc.
Pompano, Florida   1986 to present
Controller

Manage financial reporting and accounting for this $50M electronics manufacturer. Supervise and motivate staff, prepare monthly closings, complete contract negotiations, and coordinate with manufacturing to improve productivity.

• Contributed $6M to bottom line over a three year period.

• Designed and implemented a supplier consolidation program resulting in $500,000 annual savings.

SAMPLE

- Provided accounting expertise for a successful capital fund raising venture culminating in a $20M private placement.

Jamar Textiles
Houston, Texas   1984-1986
Senior Accountant

Administered all cost accounting functions for this $25M clothing manufacturer.

- Organized and implemented the organization's first standard cost system resulting in productivity increases and cost savings.

- Prepared forecasts and projections which resulted in successful financial ventures.

Carter, Inc.
Dallas, Texas   1983-1984
Accountant

Established accounting procedures for this start-up consumer products company.

- Obtained research and development credits which resulted in a $150,000 tax savings.

ACTIVITIES   Member of American Institute of CPAs
Member of Florida Institute of CPAs
Private pilot.

REFERENCES On request.

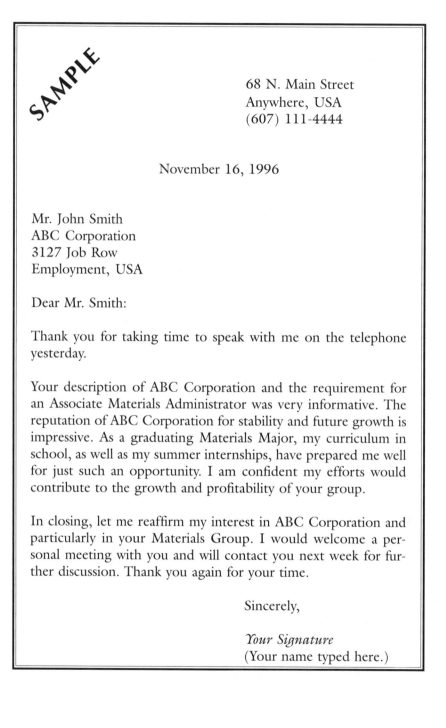

SAMPLE

68 N. Main Street
Anywhere, USA
(607) 111-4444

November 16, 1996

Mr. John Smith
ABC Corporation
3127 Job Row
Employment, USA

Dear Mr. Smith:

Thank you for taking time to speak with me on the telephone yesterday.

Your description of ABC Corporation and the requirement for an Associate Materials Administrator was very informative. The reputation of ABC Corporation for stability and future growth is impressive. As a graduating Materials Major, my curriculum in school, as well as my summer internships, have prepared me well for just such an opportunity. I am confident my efforts would contribute to the growth and profitability of your group.

In closing, let me reaffirm my interest in ABC Corporation and particularly in your Materials Group. I would welcome a personal meeting with you and will contact you next week for further discussion. Thank you again for your time.

Sincerely,

Your Signature
(Your name typed here.)

2001 Bayberry
Anywhere, USA
(415) 111-2222
November 16, 1996

Mr. John Adams
LMN Corporation
128 Career Avenue
Jenn, Missouri 64137

Dear Mr. Adams:

Thank you for your enthusiastic response to my telephone call yesterday.

Your concept of a new sales territory based here in Raleigh is exciting. As we discussed, I am very familiar with many of your potential customers and your new product sounds ideal for them. I am confident we could build this region into your number one territory within two years and I'm anxious to take on the challenge.

Thank you again for your time. I will phone you Friday morning for further discussion.

Very truly yours,

Your Signature
(Your name typed here.)

11

Designing Your Personal Marketing Campaign

B efore a new product is introduced on the market, months of planning take place. Questions such as, "What are the benefits of this product?", "Who is most likely to purchase this product?", and "How will we market this product to our prospective customers?" must be answered before a marketing campaign can be finalized.

You are now at the planning stage for a very important product: YOU. Yes, you are the product: your skills, experience, education, values, and background. Your mission is to design the best personal marketing campaign to get the word out about yourself and what you can do for others.

Fortunately, as a result of your career analysis exercises, you are already well ahead of your competition. You know yourself and you have a goal. With these clear and defined objectives, your job of developing a marketing plan is fairly simple.

A second factor in your favor: you have this book to guide you.

I Can't Sell

Some people get nervous when they are told that searching for a new job entails marketing and sales techniques. "I can't sell," they say. "I could never sell anything."

Believe me, the strategies we are about to discuss have been used successfully by many people who were adamant that they couldn't sell themselves. These same people later came back to me and admitted that once they started to use these techniques, they gained more self-confidence, and their job search actually became fun!

You *can* do it—I know you can!

Marketing Campaign Materials

Throughout your campaign, you will want to think creatively. How can you differentiate yourself from other job seekers? First, let's look at what goes into a personal marketing campaign. You need advertisements and marketing literature. We've already discussed your advertisement; that's your resume and your cover letter. Other marketing literature includes: letters of recommendation, specialized business cards, and a personal newsletter.

Letters of recommendation from people with whom you have worked or from someone who can speak about your abilities and your character are strong additions to your marketing campaign.

Specialized business cards, preferably the kind that fold in half, are a unique supplement. This style is different and it gives you more room for information. On the inside of the card, you could print your top talents and skills, and your mission statement or the objective from your resume.

You can give a card to anyone you personally meet, and you can include one when you send a thank you note and other follow-up correspondence. Most people tend to keep business cards, whereas a resume is too cumbersome to keep for a long time. If someone has your card, and two weeks after receiving it they learn of an opportunity, they can easily contact you.

(Many people have used this suggestion to their benefit. If you would like to receive a sample of the type of folding card I'm recommending, mail your request, along with your name and mailing address, to me at: 900 East Ocean Boulevard, Suite 232, Stuart, Florida 34994 or E-mail me at: twelch @ inetw.net.)

A personal newsletter, mailed once a month to everyone you've been in contact with during the course of your job search, can be beneficial. A newsletter lets people know how your search is going and it keeps your name fresh in their minds. That's the most important aspect.

I recently heard from Mark, a pharmacy director, who just relocated to Washington state from the east coast. He used the newsletter idea, and it worked very well for him. In his first newsletter he mentioned that he was planning to interview with an organization in Washington. An acquaintance who lived in Washington received the newsletter and immediately telephoned Mark to warn Mark of some problems at that organization. Not only did he warn Mark to be careful, he also said, "I didn't know you were planning a move to Washington. I know of a great opportunity. You would be perfect for the job." The rest, as they say, is history. Mark canceled his initial interview and found his perfect job—all because of a newsletter.

Marketing Methods

Now that you have your marketing materials, you'll need to choose the methods or manner in which you will search the market. The most common methods are: classified ads; the Internet; employment agen-

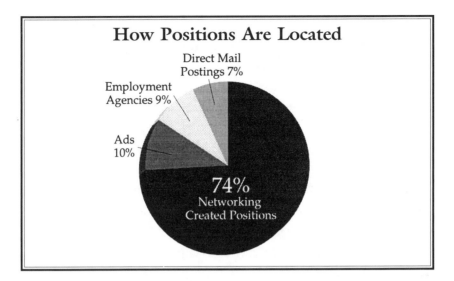

How Positions Are Located

Direct Mail Postings 7%

Employment Agencies 9%

Ads 10%

74% Networking Created Positions

cies, including temporary and interim placement; and executive search firms. Although not as popular, college placement and alumni offices, and government-backed job service offices are also used.

When people are asked, "How are you going to look for a job?" many respond, "Well, I'll read the ads in the newspaper, I'll send out my resume, and I'll contact some employment agencies." These are the least effective ways of receiving a job offer, and yet they are most people's concept of a job search plan; which is why so many people become frustrated with the process of finding employment.

Let's look at the pros and cons of each of the most commonly used job search vehicles:

Classified ads: most everyone reads the Sunday paper and sends out their resume in response to help wanted ads. You can choose to do this too, but you will have placed yourself in the mass of people who are doing the same.

Instead, you can do something different with the ad. When you see an open ad that is of interest to you (by "open" I mean the company name is provided in the ad), rather than mailing your resume to the human resource department—or whatever filter has been set up—you can use the information in the ad to locate the hiring authority. You see, oftentimes human resource personnel don't understand technical resumes. Their responsibility is to compare incoming resumes with a specification sheet given to them by the hiring manager. They are *screening out* resumes which they feel don't meet the guidelines in the specification sheet.

How do you find the name of the hiring authority? It's not difficult. (Later in this chapter I will tell you how to find their name and what to say when you have them on the telephone.) You will *not* say, "I saw your ad in the paper." That statement would land you back at human resources, which is not where you want to be. Using my approach will move you ahead of the masses. Your resume won't be in a pile four feet high. You will be different.

You can also work with ads for positions which are outside of your skills and interests. Read these ads to learn about the company and its products and services. If the company is of interest to you, contact them using the networking techniques you'll learn later in this chapter.

If you are interested in a blind ad—a company name is not provided, only a post office box is given—your only choice is to answer the ad like everyone else (unless, of course, you work for the newspaper).

However, blind or open, keep in mind that only about thirty percent of the available jobs are ever advertised in the classifieds.

The **Internet** has the largest and most diverse data base of jobs in the world, and its use as a job search tool has increased substantially in recent years. Although the Internet is a useful vehicle for posting your resume and for making contacts, it is not the ultimate job search vehicle. People are still most influenced by face-to-face communication. Getting in front of people is your most effective method.

The number of Internet sites which deal with careers and the number of online job data bases grows daily. To get started, especially if you are unfamiliar with the Internet, there are two sites which can lead you to other resources on the Internet:

1. The National Career Search and their online "Career Magazine" offers a career forum (http:\\www.careermag.com).

2. Margaret Riley's Guide will give you information on companies which have job listings online (http:\\www.wpi.edu/mfriley/jobguide.html).

Many books are available on this subject. A few suggestions are: *Mastering The Internet Job Search* by Margaret Riley, *The Online Job Search* by James Gonyea, and *Using The Internet In Your Job Search* by Fred Jandt and Mary Memnich.

If you don't own a computer, you can probably access the Internet at your local library, university, community college, or public employment service office. The U.S. Department of Labor is funding "Internet Access Zones" throughout the country at these locations.

Employment agencies and **executive search firms** are other avenues to pursue. If a couple of good firms have your name, it can be helpful in your search, but you cannot depend on them to promote your product.

Most Important Resource

Look at the graph on how people find jobs (page 149). Ten percent find jobs through the classifieds, nine percent through agencies, seven percent from direct mail postings, and a whopping seventy-four percent are from networking: the hidden market.

Therefore, when you design a personal marketing campaign, use all of these methods but concentrate your efforts in the area which has been proven to produce the best results: networking. Before you can begin to network, you'll need to develop two more lists:

1. A list of the people you know.

Hopefully, this is a long list of your friends, co-workers, relatives, teachers, business associates, neighbors, people you know from church or the laundromat or the dry cleaners, fellow parents involved with little league or school organizations, college and high school friends, etc., etc. You need to include as many people, in as many different professions, as you can. Why? Because everyone has their own circle of friends and acquaintances. I know lawyers, doctors, store clerks, dry cleaners, etc., and each of them has a different circle of people with whom they socialize or do business.

It is possible for a person outside of your profession to be very instrumental in assisting you. Let me explain:

A couple of years ago, I worked with an accountant who had lost his job. A few weeks after he and I met, he telephoned me at my office. "Do you remember all that stuff you told me?" he asked. "Well, it doesn't work. I haven't had even one interview."

"Okay," I told him, "come into my office tomorrow and we'll talk. And bring in a list of all the people you've contacted since we met."

When I reviewed his list, I saw that every person on the list was either in accounting or finance. "Bill," I said, "you have to talk with the dry cleaner, the baker—you need to talk with everyone you come in contact with, not just people in your industry." He walked out of my office with his tail between his legs. I didn't expect him to change his strategy but at least I knew his lack of success wasn't because of my advice.

The next day Bill telephoned me at my office. "I wanted to let you know that yesterday, on my way home from your office, I stopped at the same gas station I've been going to for ten years. I know the owner, not well, but at least we know each other's first names. Anyway, he comes out of the gas station and says, 'Hey Bill, how's it going?'

"And I say, 'Well, to be blunt, crummy. I lost my job two months ago, and I can't even get an interview. The economy is horrible. Life stinks.'

"'Well, what did you do?' he asked me.

"'I ran the accounting department at a little firm in the city,' I replied.

"And then he says, 'That's kind of funny, because last night at dinner my daughter said the accountant at her company left, and they have to hire someone else. Let me give you my daughter's name and phone number.'

"So, to make a long story short," says Bill, "I had an interview, and I have the job!"

Point: it is extremely important to include an awful lot of people on your list and to ask their advice.

Also realize, you will not make this list in one sitting. Don't limit yourself by association or time. Include everyone you can think of, whenever you remember their name.

2. A list of potential employers.

This list will include the companies and organizations you are interested in working for. If you want to work in a certain locale, use that area's library, Chamber of Commerce, classified ads, and yellow pages as resources. Research the area's firms to determine which companies meet your specifications.

You should base your list on the parameters which are important to you. You might consider the industry, the type of company, the size, the revenues, the location, the reputation. Whatever aspects match your interests and career values.

If you intend to consider opportunities outside of your local area, research national listings in *Standard & Poors Directory*, *The Thomas Registry*, or various other publications. Check out national classified ads in association publications or weeklies, such as the *National Business Employment Weekly*.

Research librarians can be of tremendous help to you in your market research. Tell them what you are trying to accomplish and they will guide you in the right direction.

Once you have compiled your list, try prioritizing it as best you can. List the companies you are most interested in at the top, and work your way down.

Okay. Now that you have your two lists, it's time for the fun to begin...to start networking!

Formula for people you know.

To successfully network with the people you know over the telephone, there is a five-step approach to use:

1. Identify yourself and explain why you are calling.
2. State your purpose.
3. Describe your skills.
4. Ask for their advice.
5. Ask for other contacts.

Let's say you are telephoning one of your friends on your list. Your conversation might sound like this: *Hi, Bill. This is Tom calling. I'm calling because you're a friend and I thought you could maybe give me some advice.* (You've identified yourself and explained why you are calling.) *As you might be aware, I have been affected by the downsizing at XYZ Corporation. I'm at a point in my career where I've decided to consider a new opportunity.* (You've stated your purpose.) *I know that I'm good at time management, I'm creative, and very results-oriented. I'd probably best fit in a firm's human resource department or in the marketing department of an engineering software firm.* (You've described your skills.) *Now, if you had fifteen years of experience and you were at this stage in your career, what would you do? Do you have any suggestions for me?* (You've asked for their advice.)

The advice you receive could sound like this: "You know, Tom, we have some needs in my company. Why don't you call so-and-so..." or "You know, Tom, about two years ago, I went through the same thing you're going through now. Here's what I found to be really successful..." or "Why don't you contact this person, he was really helpful to a friend of mine who was in a similar situation..."

After listening to their response and writing down the advice they give you, thank them for their help. BUT before you get off the phone, ask: *Who else do you know who might have some information that could help me?*

Hopefully, this friend will give you a couple of names that you can add to your list of potential employers or people you know.

The key to this conversation is that you ask for their advice—not if they know of a job opening. When you ask someone for a job or if they know about a job, they might be reluctant to help you. Many people are uncomfortable talking about a job...maybe they don't know what happened in your last job (why *are* you looking for work?) or they don't know what kind of an employee you are. Therefore, they might not want to discuss a specific job opening. They are hesitant to put their reputation on the line. But when you ask for their advice, they don't feel threatened. Remember, people love to give advice, especially if they think they know the subject well.

> Although people are generally reluctant to discuss a specific job opening they rarely hesitate to share their advice.

Marketing Theory 101

As you begin communicating with people about your job search, it's important for you to know that one contact is rarely enough. Since you're managing a marketing campaign, let's compare your task with that of a direct mailer. In direct mail, the rule of thumb is that to be successful, you need to mail your information to each potential customer eight times over a seventeen-month period. That's right, *eight* times. It is also said that most personal contact sales are closed on the *fifth* attempt.

My point: plan on having more than one contact with the same person. I know what you're thinking—you don't want to be a pest. And I fully agree; but there are ways for you to make numerous contacts—without being a pest.

Let's presume your initial contact with an acquaintance or a referral is a phone conversation in which they provide you with the names of two people to contact. Your second contact with your acquaintance is a thank you note for the references, along with your business card (see page 150), which you send out immediately following your first phone conversation. In this thank you note you tell them you will keep them posted on the results of your contacts with the referrals they gave you. Once you have telephoned the referrals, you can report back to your original source with the results of your conversations. (Now, you're up to three contacts with your acquaintance or referral.) Then, a couple of weeks later, you could recontact them, to provide an update on your job search and to inquire if any new ideas or names have come to their mind. With this approach, you are not being a nuisance, you're just paying attention to detail.

The fourth contact you have is very important. It is quite likely that during this time they have heard of another opportunity or they have thought of someone else for you to contact. By staying in touch, you jog their memory—without becoming a pest.

Formula for potential employers.

Before contacting potential employers, you'll need to determine how to best make contact with the hiring authority (the person who would be your boss) in the department you are interested in. You don't want to spend your energy on people who can't hire you, like the human resource department. As much as human resource departments are needed, typically they do not have the authority to hire. You can go into a human resource department and ask if they have a job for you. The response will be, "No, I'm sorry we do not have any requisitions." This department can tell you "no" but they can't tell you "yes."

> You *can* avoid the frustration of answering ads and sending out your resume or depending on employment agencies and human resource departments.

Who can tell you "yes?" The hiring authority in your area. Since eighty percent of the hiring decision is based on personality, how can you get to the hiring authority and show them your personality? Fortunately, there are a few different ways to make contact with a hiring authority:

1. Check with a friend who works at the company. Ask them for the name of the hiring authority for your area. Your friend might also provide some insight about the hiring authority and give you suggestions on how to best approach them. If appropriate, you could also inquire about using your friend's name as an introductory reference.

2. Call the switchboard operator and ask who is the director of the department. Nine times out of ten the operator will give you their name. If the operator or receptionist asks why you are calling, say, "I don't really need to speak to them. I have some correspondence I want to send to them. Can you give me their name and mailing address?" (This information will come in handy if you later need to send them your resume.)

"Oh, sure..." says the operator.

Then, the next day you telephone the company and ask to speak with the director of the department by name.

3. Call a department which deals with the public, like accounts payable, customer service, or marketing and sales. They are accustomed to calls from outsiders and will often provide you with a name. When someone answers the phone, you can say, "I wonder if you might answer a question for me. I'm trying to reach the Director of Engineering. What is his or her name?"

If they don't know, ask, "Is there someone else in the area who might know?" If not, "Could you please transfer my call to the Engineering Department?" When someone in Engineering answers the phone, ask for the name of the director.

Don't be intimidated by this approach. Oftentimes, you will be doing the hiring authority (your potential boss) a favor by getting in touch with them. Maybe there is an employee in their department who isn't working out as expected. The manager would like to replace this employee, but that would entail placing an advertisement, reviewing resumes, holding interviews, etc. Instead of going through the hassle of finding a replacement, they'll keep the employee who isn't performing at one hundred percent. However, if *you* introduce yourself over the phone, and you have the personality and the skills they want...then the manager can do something with the current employee and bring you in. That's part of the hidden job market.

Or maybe when you speak with the manager, they will say, "You know, I can't really help you but if you talk to Ken Jones, he works in our software development department, he needs someone like you. I suggest you call him. Here's his number."

Ninety percent of the time, it should be that easy for you to get through to the hiring authority. For the other ten percent, you'll need to know how to bypass the gatekeepers.

4. Getting past the gatekeepers takes some skill, but nothing you can't learn with practice. You've determined who your hiring authority most likely is. How do you contact them? How do you get past their secretary's question, "Is he expecting your call?"

You respond, "No, but he will be happy I phoned."

"What's the purpose of your call?" she continues.

"I have some technical information to discuss with him," you insist. (The technical information is your background and skills. Of course you don't mention that you are looking for a job, because then the secretary will have you transferred to the *human resource department*.) Or you could say, "I need his advice on a technical matter."

This response should get you past the secretary. Believe me, once you've practiced it a few times, working with secretaries will be easy. If the manager is not available, usually the secretary will ask if you would like to leave a message. My recommendation is that you do *not* leave a message. When you leave a message, you turn control over to someone else. If you don't hear back from them in a timely fashion, you might be reluctant to call them again, for fear of being a pest. Here's a better way:

Secretary: "I'm sorry, Mrs. Donovan isn't available. May I give her a message?"

You: "Thank you for asking but I'm on my way out. It would be best if I phoned her back. Is there a time that's better than another to reach her?" (Now, you're still in control.)

Secretary: "Let's see, she has a meeting at one-thirty, and she's normally back from lunch by one. Why don't you try to catch her between one and one-thirty?"

You: "I'll try again about one-fifteen. Thank you for your help."

Always treat secretaries with respect. They can be a big help to you, and also a wealth of information.

Before you know it, you'll have the hiring authority on the telephone. Then, what do you say? You follow this five step approach:

1.   Identify yourself.
2.   Explain why you're calling.
3.   Describe your skills.
4.   Ask for their advice.
5.   Ask for other contacts.

Your conversation could sound like this: *Hello. This is Tom Welch. I'm calling because your company has an excellent reputation and it was suggested that I contact you.* (You've identified yourself and explained why you are calling him.) If the hiring authority questions who referred you to him, you can respond: *Well, the person who told me asked that I keep their name confidential. But if they don't mind me telling you later, I'll be glad to share that information with you then.* All questions about your source will stop there. You continue: *I have fifteen years experience in software development. I'm really good at time management, I'm cre-ative, and very results-oriented.* (You've described your skills.) *Now, if you were at this stage in your career, and knowing what you do about the industry, what would you do? Can you give me any suggestions?* (You've asked for their advice.) Even though it is an unspoken understanding, you haven't actually asked for a job.

Their advice could be, "Gee, we have some needs in our organiza-tion" or "We don't have any openings here, actually we are laying off staff ourselves, however, I attended a conference last week and so-and-so was looking for someone with your skills..." After listening to their advice and writing it down, you thank them for their help. And **before** you get off the phone, ask: *Is there anyone else you know, either socially or through your business, whom I should contact for suggestions?*

You're now reaching people who can make a difference in your job search. You're establishing an expanding network to market yourself in.

Practice-Practice-Practice

When you first start telephoning potential employers (and the people you know), your telephone skills will be rusty. In fact, you probably won't be very good—but with practice, you will be great. Therefore, when you look at your list of potential employers, start by telephoning the companies at the bottom of your list. Practice your interview skills on them, since they are least important to you. Then, by the time you reach the top of your list (the companies you'd *really* like to join), your skills are top-notch. In the beginning, you can even write your script out, but I promise that after you've done this five or ten times, you won't need a piece of paper.

This is the beginning of your network. It requires a lot of phone time; but it's worth it.

Handling Rejection

Rejection is a part of any marketing campaign—and you will experience your share of it during your job search. Not everyone will say, "Hey,

I'm so glad you phoned. Boy, we sure could use you in the department. Come on down and let's talk."

You will be told, "No. No, I don't have the time to talk today. Why are you calling? Who are you?"

However, if you realize ahead of time that throughout this process you will experience rejection, then you can prepare yourself for it and lessen your frustration. (Remember, there really is no such thing as rejection, only actions and results. See Chapter 7.) Successful people know how to manage frustration and rejection. Here's a true story about a man you've heard about before

> In his twenties, he was a drifter. When he turned thirty-one, he decided he needed to do something with his life, so he formed a business partnership. One-and-a-half years later he went bankrupt and lost everything. Since he was broke, he decided he might as well enter politics. In his first local election, he lost badly. Two years later, at the age of thirty-four, he decided to go back into business. What happened? He went bankrupt, again. A year later, things were looking up; he fell in love with a beautiful woman. What happened? She died. At the age of thirty-six he had a nervous breakdown and was confined to his bed for months. Finally, he shook off his depression, and two years later he decided to run for Congress. He lost. At forty-six he ran for Congress again; and lost. At the age of forty-eight, he decided to run for the Senate. He lost that election as well. When he was fifty-five years old, he tried to win his party's nomination for the vice presidency; he didn't. At fifty-eight, he ran for the Senate again, and lost. Finally, at sixty years of age, Abraham Lincoln was elected to the office of President of the United States.

Did he let frustration get him down? No. Did he let depression set in? I don't think so.

I guarantee that if you follow the strategies in this book, you will succeed at finding increased joy and fulfillment. The path will not always be smooth, but if you keep focused on your mission and follow your marketing plan, you will succeed. Successful people have these four things in common:

1. **A Goal** (You want the right job.)
2. **A Belief They Can Accomplish Their Goal** (You know you have strong skills and talents. You know they are valuable, and you believe you will find the right job.)
3. **A Specific Plan To Accomplish Their Goal** (You are establishing your marketing plan now.)
4. **Action** (You will do what it takes to obtain your goal. You will take control and change your job and your life.)

Someone once said, "Anything worth doing is worth doing poorly, because at least you're doing something; and you learn by doing."

If you take action, what will you get? Results. Will the results always be what you anticipated? No. What do you do if your action doesn't produce the result you wanted? You must alter your action or take a different action entirely. And, if that doesn't get your desired result, you keep on revising your actions until you achieve the result you wanted. Once you get the result you were after, you keep taking that same action over and over again—because you know it works.

I'm going to share a secret with you. Because I've been doing this for so long, I can help you circumvent most of the frustration people feel when looking for a job. You're not going to have to test, test, test. You can avoid the frustration of answering classified ads and sending out your resume, or depending on employment agencies and human resource departments. I'm going to save you time, effort, and money because this book is full of successful formulas.

Too many people stop right here. They do all of the exercises in this book. They believe in themselves. They design a personal marketing plan. They take action—and the result isn't what they expected—so they stop. Don't say, "I can't do this." You must keep telephoning people.

You must keep talking with people. You must be committed to marketing yourself six to eight hours a day.

A while ago I worked with two men in their fifties. They were both engineering managers. One man worked two jobs in Europe, then he was transferred to the United States by his company. He worked in the states for eight years and then one day he was suddenly laid off. The other man had worked for one company most of his life, when he was recruited by another company. He worked for them for one year, and he was laid off.

Both of these men were feeling useless and depressed. As I counseled them on their careers, we went through the job search exercises in this book.

Afterwards, they both began their job search. Within a week, both men contacted me to say they were having so much FUN contacting people and potential employers that they would be a little disappointed once they accepted a new position! They were getting positive responses over the phone, and their self-esteem had improved dramatically. People were expressing an interest in their skills and experience.

The same thing will happen to you when you take the action to make it happen.

Obtaining The Interview

Throughout your marketing campaign, your goal is to obtain an interview with the hiring authority. You want the hiring authority to meet you face-to-face, to further cement the rapport you established over the telephone.

Speaking of phone conversations, you only have about thirty seconds of someone's attention before they start to drift. Therefore, before you pick up the telephone, be sure you know what you are going to say. Know the name of the company, the title and name of the person you want to talk with, and be in a positive frame of mind.

When you talk on the phone, smile. You can't sound angry or upset when you smile. Smiling makes your voice sound enthusiastic.

Be assertive; not pushy. And remember, never leave messages! If you left a message and the person doesn't return your call, you can't call them again without having the dilemma of being "pushy." However, if you haven't left a message, there is no dilemma.

> I was trying to contact a potential client. I tried forever and ever and I could never get him on the phone. Finally, one night I was in my office at 6:15 p.m., and I thought, "I'm going to call him now."
>
> I dialed his number, and before the phone even rang twice, I hear in the receiver, "I know. You need the bread and the milk. I'm just about ready to leave. Is there anything else?"
>
> Of course, after I identified myself, we laughed...and we've been doing business together ever since.

I couldn't reach him during normal business hours. You might try to reach a manager before the secretary arrives at 8:00 a.m. or 8:30 a.m. or try after 5:00 p.m. Many managers will pick up their own phones outside of the normal business day.

As you take action, opportunities will present themselves. Be persistent. If you feel you're getting into a rut or you're not handling rejection well, go back and read this chapter. You can overcome whatever frustration you encounter.

These strategies work. When you've been successful and you're invited for an interview, you will be getting ever nearer to your destination: a job offer. However keep in mind that the job doesn't always go to the most qualified individual. It goes to the person who makes the *best presentation*. What can you do so that you are the one who makes the best presentation? I'll give you those tips next.

Part Four

Winning
The Interview

12

Winning The Interview Game

The interview is the single most important part of your job search because it is where you can sell yourself to the hiring authority and it is where you can evaluate the company as a potential employer. You should not let the thought of going to an interview overwhelm you. An interview is simply face to face communication, between two parties, initiated for a specific purpose. In this chapter we will take an in-depth look at how you can succeed at interviewing.

Research The Company

If you are genuinely interested in a position and you want a chance at receiving a job offer, there are three common mistakes you must avoid: not knowing *why* you are interested in the job, not being sure of your *interest* in the company, and not being able to communicate your *expec-*

tations of the job. Any one of these errors could easily cost you a job offer.

The easiest way to avoid these mistakes is to research the company prior to your interview. Learn about the company's products and services by:

Reading their annual reports, newsletters, and product brochures. You can locate information on most large corporations from the following sources:

- ❑ Better Business Bureau
- ❑ Chamber of Commerce
- ❑ Moody's Manuals
- ❑ Dun & Bradstreet Reference Book
- ❑ MacRae's Bluebook
- ❑ Fitch Corporations Manuals
- ❑ Standard and Poor's publications
- ❑ Thomas' Register of American Manufacturers
- ❑ *Fortune's* Annual List of Top 500 companies
- ❑ College Placement Directory (Zimmerman & Lavine)
- ❑ College Placement Annual (College Placement Council)

Talk to the company's customers. Ask them questions like: "What is your impression of the company?", "Are they stable?", "Are they growing?", and "How would you rate their customer service?"

Interview current and past employees. Find out if the company is a good organization to work for.

Ask the company's competitors for their opinion.

By learning as much as you can about the company prior to the interview, you will have a better understanding of the position you are seeking and your knowledge of the company will be evident during the interview. I guarantee this enthusiasm and interest will make an impact on the hiring authority.

Mock Interview

When you've completed your research of the company, run through a mock interview with a friend or an instructor. Have them ask you some of the most-frequently asked interview questions (see pages 176 and 187)—and any other questions they think are relevant to the position you are interviewing for. If possible, videotape the mock interview, so you can critique your performance. Remember, eighty percent of the job offers made are based on personality and rapport...which is strongly influenced by body language.

First Impressions

People will make more assumptions about you within the first thirty seconds of meeting you than they will during the rest of your visit. If you make a great first impression, it will be very difficult for you to undo the positive feelings you created. Conversely, if you make a poor first impression, you could have an extremely difficult time repairing the damage.

How can you make a great first impression? Be on time for the interview. Be polite, confident, sincere, and enthusiastic. Make eye contact. Smile. Have a firm handshake. Remember the names of people you meet.

You must make a good impression on everyone you meet. There could be more than one decision maker involved in the hiring process, so you don't want to offend anyone.

Here's how one man failed to make a good first impression and ruined his chances for the job:

A man who was interested in being a director of production for a large company was running late for his interview. As he arrived at the entrance, he saw that the company had a security guard stationed at the door. The man ran up to the entrance, very agitated.

Per custom, the security guard started to ask him standard questions: "What's your name?", "Can I have your license plate number?", "Who are you here to see?", etc.

"Come on. I gotta get out of here," snaps the man, as he

rushes past the security guard. "I'm late for my interview. I don't have time for these questions."

Immediately, the security guard phones the production department. "Who is this clown you're expecting?..." The guard explains the rudeness he has just encountered.

This man's chances of a job offer were ruined before he even stepped foot into the building. Why? Because he made a poor first impression on the security guard.

The Interview

To succeed at an interview, you must do so many things right. Remember my analogy about a smooth-running engine? It really holds true at this point in your job search. You've worked so hard to get an interview, don't get sloppy now. Take the time to study these critical interview points. If you follow these guidelines, you'll have a successful interview.

❧ Be on time for the interview. ☙
Don't make others wait for you. You could lose the opportunity to even have the interview.

❧ Be courteous. ☙
No one wants to be around someone who is rude, impolite, or belligerent. Be on your best behavior.

❧ Be well-groomed. ☙
Dress your best. Show that you care about your appearance. Remember that first impression?

❧ Build rapport. ☙
During an interview it is critical that you build rapport. As soon as you meet the interviewer, you must make them feel comfortable with you.

What Employers Look For On Applications:

1. Gaps in employment history.
2. Reasons for leaving jobs.
3. Insufficient responses.
4. Inconsistencies.
5. Plans for the future.
6. Likes and dislikes.
7. Ability to follow directions.

The more they like you as a person, the greater your chance of receiving an offer.

I know. Everyone is different. Personalities vary. Attitudes differ. How can you control whether a person likes you or not? Here's the secret: people tend to like people who are similar to them. And people tend to make a judgement about another person rather quickly. So, in the first few minutes of your interview, be as much like the interviewer as you can.

The factor which most contributes to the "Do I like you?" decision is body language. Notice how the interviewer sits. Watch for gestures and eye contact. Follow the lead of the interviewer and adjust your body language accordingly.

Next, listen to the tone of their speech. Is it loud or soft, fast or slow? Your tone should be similar. Tune in to their vocabulary. Use the same words and phrases.

I am not suggesting that you become someone you are not. This communications technique is an equalizer you can use at the outset of a conversation. Once rapport is established, do what is comfortable for you. In order to work happy and live healthy, you have to be yourself. But if you can build a high level of rapport early in the interview, the remainder of your meeting will be much easier, and you can expect positive results. If you don't build rapport, the outcome could be very different.

I knew a man who was interviewing for the position of director of quality control. He had already interviewed with several managers and all of them highly recommended this man for the position. He had only one more interview—with the general manager.

During his interview with the general manager, the man felt intimidated. He was unable to maintain eye contact, he kept looking down. Even though all of the managers felt he was perfect for the position, the general manager said, "No. I'm not going to hire him. If he can't look me in the eye, how will he communicate with his staff?"

For that one reason—poor eye contact—the man did not receive the job offer.

DOs And DON'Ts For A Successful Interview

DO...	DON'T...
act naturally. Shake hands firmly.	arrive late or miss the interview.
smile.	be tense.
arrive on time. Be courteous.	criticize yourself.
build rapport.	present an extreme appearance.
ask relevant questions.	become impatient or emotional.
give the employer a chance to express their views.	answer questions with a simple "yes" or "no."
be prepared to answer questions.	oversell your case.
communicate clearly.	lie.
show interest and enthusiasm.	talk too much or too little.
believe in yourself.	become intimidated.
explain how your skills and experience are relevant to the job opportunity.	make derogatory remarks about your present or former boss or company.
sell yourself and close the sale.	give undue consideration to negotiating salary in the first interview.

✧ Listen well. ✧

Good listening skills are essential to successful communication. Effective listening takes practice and concentration.

The average person speaks between 120 and 200 words per minute; yet we can comprehend between 600 and 800 words per minute. Thus, most of us have a tendency to let our minds drift during meetings.

Being prepared for the interview will make effective listening easier. If you're ready to answer questions and you are knowledgeable about the company, you'll be better able to include personal sales features into your answers. The interview will flow more easily, from start to finish.

✧ Accent the positive. ✧

Don't degrade yourself. Turn any potentially negative response into a positive remark.

✧ Don't condemn past employers. ✧

You never want to criticize either the company you worked for or a former supervisor. The interviewer could interpret your negative remarks as a sign that this is what you would say about them.

✧ Interview the interviewer. ✧

You will be judged by how you answer questions asked of you, as well as by the questions you ask. If you don't show interest, by asking appropriate questions, it could be used as a strike against you.

Remember, you're trying to sell yourself. If the interviewer doesn't ask the right questions, you won't be able to discuss your skills and talents. Be prepared to take control so that your selling points can be made. During the interview, you must identify your top five or six skills, either by preparing answers to expected questions or by posing your own questions to the interviewer. For instance, a simple question like, "Would my ability to meet several deadlines at once be an asset in this position?" or "Does my ability to work well with varied personality types help?"

Why Interviewers Ask Questions

The Employment Management Association surveyed a group of executives to learn what questions they most-frequently asked job candidates, and why they asked the questions. Below are their responses:

1. *Why are you interested in this position? or Why did you respond to our ad?*
   Answers reflect pre-interview preparation, including knowledge of the industry and the company; a clarification of goals, including job priorities; and likes and dislikes.

2. *Tell me about your previous bosses. What kind of people were they?*
   Answers indicate personality traits, maturity, and potential conflicts.

3. *Has your job performance ever been evaluated? How were you assessed?*
   Answers will reflect your honesty. While no one is expected to reveal major flaws, everyone has a weakness. A failure to admit a weakness gives a negative impression.

4. *What were the most satisfying aspects of prior jobs? The most frustrating?*
   Answers indicate character traits. Is the candidate results-oriented and pleased with the attainment of specific goals? Conversely, have there been personal conflicts which stymied efforts to reach objectives?

5. *Describe a time when you felt ineffective, why you felt ineffective, what you did about it, and what the outcome was.*
   Again, the interviewer is trying to identify behavior traits. If the candidate forgets to answer part two, three, or four of the question, it usually indicates a short attention span and poor attention to detail.

6. *Describe a time when you felt particularly effective.*
   More than the activity itself, the interviewer is interested in how the activity is described and the behavior evidenced during the explanation. If the job candidate says, "I'm not sure what you want," they may have a dependent personality.

7. *Were your assignments handled individually or were they a team effort?*
   The interviewer tries to determine whether the job candidate will exaggerate about their influence in performing tasks and achieving results. The question seeks a balance.

8. *What are the most important factors you require in a job? How should a job be structured to best satisfy you?*
   The interviewer is looking for consistency and is trying to determine how well the job candidate might adapt to their company.

9. *Where do you want to be in the next five to ten years?*
   Use this open-ended question to sell your particular skills and abilities.

When you ask questions, you can seek information about the company and the position. You can evaluate the hiring authority's personality, and it gives the interviewer time to talk. You can learn a lot by listening to what the interviewer has to say about the company.

⤳ Tell the truth. ⤳

Although I've used the word "performance," I am *not* suggesting you put on an act during the interview. Be yourself. Don't tell little white lies or hide or fabricate information. If you feel the need to provide false information, so that you look more attractive to the interviewer, the job isn't the right one for you.

⤳ Provide specific information. ⤳

Answer questions directly and give examples of your achievements. Specific details lend credibility to your capabilities. For example, if an interviewer asks why you think you're a good machinist, rather than responding, "Well, people have told me that I am good," you should say: "Let me tell you why I am a good machinist. I've worked in the trade for fifteen years and I've never missed a day of work. I've never been late, either. I've designed new processes...I'm always trying to devise a better way to do things. Let me give you an example of something I did. My previous employer was trying to find a better way to do this process. To help, I talked with other machinists, some of the supervisors, and the foremen. After chatting with these people, I came up with a concept...and we got it done."

You have provided a specific example. Remember, you are selling yourself. You need to be more assertive when answering questions.

⤳ Mention the company name. ⤳

If you are interviewing at Motorola, mention "Motorola" several times during the interview. For instance, "Are Motorola's benefits similar to this?" or "Is this the policy that Motorola usually follows?" A job candidate who mentions the company name receives more job offers.

↜ Use action-oriented language. ↝

Eliminate passive words and phrases from your speech. Don't be meek or humble. Express how you can contribute to the company and how you can solve problems. If you are asked, "Are you dedicated to your employer?" don't respond, "Yeah. I'm a pretty dedicated employee." Instead say, "Yes. I'm very dedicated. Let me give you an example..."

↜ Analyze the job. ↝

Try to evaluate the hiring authority and the company. Do they meet your expectations and objectives? Carefully examine the position itself. Will you be challenged? Is there potential for future growth? What is the general attitude of the office? Will your values be met? Speak with the employees, to get their opinions.

↜ Be prepared to provide references. ↝

You should select at least three people (past employers, supervisors, instructors, etc.) whom you can use as references. These people should be prepared to respond to telephone inquiries from potential employers.

A personal reference can supply valuable and objective information about your qualifications. The people you choose as references should be able to offer facts regarding your:

- ❑ motivational level
- ❑ energy level
- ❑ leadership abilities
- ❑ ability to meet deadlines
- ❑ judgement and common sense
- ❑ aptitude
- ❑ attitudes and personality
- ❑ relationships with people
- ❑ accuracy and work speed

After a potential employer has asked you for references, it is essential that you recontact your references to tell them that they should expect a phone call from the potential employer. Also, advise your references of any particular facts you feel they should know about each position you interview for.

What The Manager Is Trying To Discover About You

JOB KNOWLEDGE AND EXPERIENCE
Previous Positions Held

EDUCATION AND SKILLS

Secondary School   Vocational Schooling
College Degrees   Special Training & Courses

CHARACTER

Reliability   Integrity
Honesty

INTELLECTUAL

Ability to Communicate   Judgement
Mental Ability   Flexibility and Adaptability
Aptitudes

PERSONALITY

Initiative and Drive   Values: Job and General
Self Confidence   Interests and Leisure Activities
Emotional Stability   Sociability: Friendliness
Aspiration Level   Cooperation
Reaction to Pressure   Sense of Humor
Motivational Level   Personal Insight

ENVIRONMENT

Family Obligations   Financial Obligations

PHYSICAL QUALIFICATIONS

Appearance   Health

↵ Be flexible on salary. ↩

If you are asked what salary you would accept, reply that you would prefer that they extend an offer to you, based on their evaluation of you. (See Chapter 13.)

↵ Close the sale. ↩

Too many job applicants have a good interview, and then leave without asking for the job. If the job is of interest, don't end your interview by saying, "No, I don't have any more questions. Thank you for your time." Be assertive. Close the sale.

If you want the job, say, "You know, I do have one more question. We've had a great visit today. I really appreciate the time you've taken to meet with me. I feel extremely confident that I can do what you need done. When can I start?"

Wow! What a different approach. The interviewer just might say, "How about next Monday?"! Even if they don't say that, at least you have expressed great enthusiasm over the job. You tried to close the sale.

Maybe the interviewer will reply, "Well, before I can answer your question, I need to think about it."

While you are still face-to-face with the interviewer, find out how they feel about you. Rather than accept a response like this from the interviewer, try to find out where you really stand: "Would you mind if I asked you one more question?"

"No, go ahead," the interviewer says.

"Well, we talked about my abilities and my experience. Is that what you need to think about?"

"Oh, no. I feel you have everything we need for this position," confirms the interviewer.

"I mentioned that I couldn't start for two weeks, because of commitments I have. Is that what you need to think about?" you pursue.

"No. The timing would work out well," assures the interviewer.

"We talked a bit about salary. Is that what you need to think about?" you ask.

"Yeah," admits the interviewer, "that's what I need to think about." (See Chapter 13 for tips on discussing salary.)

You finally identified the problem. If you had left without questioning the interviewer, you might never have learned what the dilemma was, and two weeks later you would receive notification that someone else was hired—and you wouldn't understand why.

Once you've left the interview, it is too easy for the interviewer to hide why they selected someone else for the position. Rather than admitting they couldn't afford you, they might say something like, "We found someone who was a little more qualified." But by identifying the problem at the interview stage, you can reopen the discussion, maybe resolve the issue, and still receive an offer.

> I knew a man who was a vice president of human resources. He was interviewing with the executive vice president of a corporation. At the end of the interview, he said, "Yes, I do have one more question. We had a really good visit today. I am extremely confident that I can come in here and make a contribution to your company. When can I start?"
>
> "You know," said the executive vice president, "I've interviewed five finalists for this position and you're the first one to ask me that. I'm going to hire you."

He closed the sale and received the offer. Some hiring authorities need to be pulled into a decision—and all they need is a little encouragement from you.

The Employer's View

During the interview, the hiring authority is analyzing what you say and how you act, to determine if you would be good for the position. There are seven areas most employers consider when screening job candidates:

- ❑ Your ability to adjust to the job environment.
- ❑ The likelihood of supervisors and co-workers accepting you.
- ❑ Your ability to perform the work.
- ❑ Your interest in doing the job.
- ❑ The likelihood that you will remain with the company.
- ❑ Your potential for further growth.

❑ Your ability to keep personal matters from interfering with your job performance.

As the employer determines how you rate in those seven areas, they are also watching and listening for any negative "flags." Below are some negative behaviors you should avoid displaying during an interview. This list, compiled by the Northwestern Endicott Report, is based on a survey of 153 companies:

❑ Poor personal appearance.

❑ Overbearing, aggressive, or "superior" attitude. A "know-it-all."

❑ Inability to express yourself clearly: poor voice, diction, and grammar.

❑ Lack of planning for career: no purpose or goals.

❑ Lack of interest and enthusiasm: passive and indifferent demeanor.

❑ Lack of confidence and poise: nervousness.

❑ Failure to participate in leisure time activities.

❑ Overemphasis on money.

❑ Poor scholastic record or marked dislike for school.

❑ Unwillingness to start at the bottom: expect too much too soon.

❑ Evasiveness: hedging on unfavorable issues.

❑ Lack of tact or maturity.

❑ Lack of courtesy: ill mannered.

❑ Condemnation of past employers.

❑ Lack of social understanding.

❑ Lack of vitality.

❑ Failure to look interviewer in the eye.

❑ Limp, fishy handshake.

❑ Indecisiveness.

❑ Friction with parents.

❑ Sloppy job application or resume.

❑ Disinterest in position and/or company. Admission of merely shopping around.

❑ Desire to keep job for only a short time.

❑ Little sense of humor.

❑ Lack of knowledge in the field.

❑ No interest shown in company or industry.

❑ Emphasis on "who" you know.

❑ Unwillingness to travel.

❑ Cynicism.

❑ Low moral standards.

❑ Laziness.

❑ Intolerance and strong prejudices.

❑ Narrow interests.

❑ Poor handling of personal finances.

❑ No interest in community activities.

❑ Inability to handle criticism.

❑ Radical ideas.

❑ Arriving late to the interview without a valid reason.

❑ Failure to ask questions about the job or company.

❑ Vague answers to questions.

⤳ Follow-up Communication. ⤳

If you left the interview without a firm job offer, it is imperative that you write a letter to the hiring authority, thanking them for their time and interest. In this follow-up letter, mention highlights of the interview, and reemphasize how your education and/or experience could solve the company's problem or contribute to the company's success. Reiterate that you were impressed with the company and that you would like to prove your worth. The hiring authority should receive this letter the day following your interview. Even if you have to use express mail or hand deliver the letter, it should arrive the *next* day. This speed will reemphasize your enthusiasm and interest.

What if the interviewer told you that final interviews were going to be conducted next Tuesday and that a group decision would be made after that? You should still send a follow-up letter, and on next Wednesday you should telephone the interviewer to say, "I just wanted to let you know one more thing. When I left your facility last Friday, I was extremely interested in the job. I've now had four nights to sleep on it, and I'm even more interested today. I just wanted to let you know that." You haven't put pressure on the hiring authority by asking, "Have you made a decision yet?" But you have put yourself back in the forefront of their mind—where the last job candidates were. This can be a very beneficial follow-up activity.

⤳ Post-Interview Critique. ⤳

Your objective is to improve with each interview you have. By evaluating yourself after every interview, you will, in fact, get better. Following each interview, ask yourself these questions:

❑   Was I prepared for the interview?

❑   Was I at ease?

❑   Was rapport established?

❑   Did I ask questions?

❑ Did I listen well? Was I able to concentrate?

❑ Did I sell myself well?

❑ Did I ask for the job?

❑ How can I improve?

❑ Am I satisfied with the general results?

❑ Did I follow-up?

The Offer

If you follow these strategies, you will find yourself in the enviable position of receiving an offer of employment. When you receive the offer, you'll know you excelled in the interview. You made a great presentation and you should be proud of yourself.

But don't relax just yet. Now it's your turn to make a decision. Each offer you receive must be evaluated, based on the goals you've set for yourself. You must consider all aspects of the job and compare them with the skills you enjoy using most and your career values. Before accepting an offer, you must know:

❑ What is the exact position that is being offered, including its title and responsibilities?

❑ How does the department and job fit into the company's structure?

❑ What are the opportunities for advancement?

❑ Have there been any recent organizational changes?

❑ What became of your predecessor?

❑ As your responsibilities grow, can the position be upgraded?

❑ How does the company evaluate job performances?

The more you know about the company and the position, the easier your decision will be. Remember, the simple Job Success Formula:

1. use the skills and talents you enjoy using,
2. where your values are met and
3. you feel you are making a difference.

You have the tools to accurately predict whether or not this offer is right for you. As you think about the position and what it requires, review your talents and skills. Will the job allow you to use your most enjoyable skills? Go back over your list of career values. Will those values be met by the company and the job? Does the job excite you? Does it match your interests to the extent that you know, without a doubt, that you will be able to make a difference?

If you answer yes to all three elements of the Job Success Formula, your decision is easy. If certain elements are missing, contemplate carefully before making a decision. Maybe you could negotiate different aspects of the job to make it more appealing. Once you have the initial offer, it is the perfect time to use the finer points of negotiating to your best advantage. It's easy to do—I'll show you how.

Most-Frequently Asked Interview Questions

- ❏ Why should we hire you?
- ❏ Do you like routine work?
- ❏ What is your major strength/weakness?
- ❏ Why do you want to work for us?
- ❏ How would you describe yourself?
- ❏ How do you work under pressure?
- ❏ What types of people irritate you?
- ❏ What do you know about our organization?
- ❏ Do you prefer working regular or irregular hours?
- ❏ What are the disadvantages of working in your field?
- ❏ Are you greatly concerned about pleasing other people?
- ❏ What qualifications do you have for this job?
- ❏ Would you rather work for a small or a large company? Why?
- ❏ Do you prefer working in a specific geographic location? Why?
- ❏ What personal characteristics are necessary to succeed in your field?
- ❏ If given the opportunity to choose, which position in our company would you prefer?
- ❏ Are you willing to travel?
- ❏ What is the most important thing you've learned from your previous jobs?
- ❏ How do you usually spend your weekends?
- ❏ What types of magazines and books do you usually read?
- ❏ What two or three accomplishments have given you the most satisfaction? Why?
- ❏ What two or three things are most important to you in your job?

13

Negotiation: Getting The Most For You

You deserve to enjoy your job. You deserve a job which makes work seem like play. You deserve a career which meets your values and matches your skills. You deserve to wake up in the morning, and instead of going to work, you go to life.

Unfortunately, jobs like this don't just fall in your lap. They are out there, but sometimes you have to create them. You might have to modify an initial job offer, to make the job meet your needs. And that is where negotiation skills enter the picture.

Successful negotiating depends on you, and your inner resources. You *can* be a great negotiator, if you have: a desire to make it happen, a knowledge of the negotiation process, and the inner drive to take the necessary actions to produce the results you're after.

You cannot rely on other people to shape your life or your career. It depends on you.

Many people have a narrow view of negotiation and find the whole process discomforting. They view it as one party trying to outdo the other. You don't want to leave an interview feeling as though you've been taken advantage of, had no input, or no control. And you certainly don't want to feel like you were coerced into agreeing to something you didn't want.

What if you could look forward to negotiating? What if you could remove all of the discomfort from the process, and focus on what you could gain rather than what you could lose? The principles I will share with you have been taught to thousands of people who have successfully used them to negotiate compensation packages they never thought possible.

First, you must understand that negotiating the best deal is not an event which happens at the end of an interview; it is a process which can begin long before an interview occurs. Negotiations begin whenever you make your first impression on the company, whether it is by mailing your resume, making a telephone call, or sending a video tape.

Second, during the interview you want to establish open communication, and an atmosphere of cooperation which seeks a balance for both you and the hiring authority. Your discussion should be honest and relaxed. You don't have to play the old game of "high-low:" where you start high, the employer starts low, and somewhere in the middle there is an agreeable solution. You can keep your values without sacrificing your integrity. You can be fair, while assertively trying to satisfy your needs.

Third, a willingness to give, rather than simply take, will produce a fair balance. When your interests and those of the employer are heard and understood, then both of your needs can be met in the best possible way. The process of negotiating becomes simple:

❑ You will feel more comfortable and less stressed.
❑ The employer will feel more at ease.
❑ There is a more honest exchange of information.

❑ Both you and the employer will feel confident that the agreement has merit for both sides.

❑ You will have a job that matches your skills and values.

❑ You will begin your new job with positive feelings.

This chapter will help you understand and practice proven negotiation strategies. By developing a high level of confidence in your negotiating skills, you will empower yourself to earn all that you're worth.

You Can Get What You Want

If you don't ask for what you want, chances are you won't get it. Simple, right? Unfortunately, when it comes to our livelihoods, it is often difficult for us to muster up the courage to ask for what we want. Instead, we ask ourselves doubting questions like, "What if the employer gets turned off by my approach?" or "Am I worth what I think I'm worth?" Fortunately, it's easy to learn how to make the negotiating process work on your behalf.

When you hear the word "negotiate" do you get negative thoughts in your mind? If you do, you can change your way of thinking. Do not equate *negotiation* with *confrontation*. You are not out to get as much as possible while giving as little as possible. Think of negotiating as brainstorming: how can you and the employer create the best deal for both parties?

When you view negotiation positively, you will begin to associate pleasure with the whole process. This will make you more effective and the negotiations will be a win-win situation. To reach this positive state, ask yourself positive questions:

❑ "How will I feel when I negotiate so well that I get paid what I am worth?"

❑ "How proud will I be when we reach a mutually-beneficial agreement?"

❑　"When I interview and negotiate effectively, how much more will I enjoy my work?"

⤳ Setting The Tone ⤳

During the interview you should be congenial, confident, flexible, open, honest, and straightforward. Act and speak enthusiastically. These traits will not only help the employer make you an offer, they will carry over into the salary negotiations.

Let the hiring authority know that your intent is to reach a mutually-beneficial agreement. Yes, you are motivated by a need for self preservation, but you will achieve greater success and maximize your professional worth, through a cooperative effort rather than an effort which pulls you and the hiring authority apart. Preserve the relationship you built during the earlier stages of the interview. The rapport you established is critical.

Always remain objective when presenting your requests. Do not let your emotions get in the way of rational thinking. Sometimes, since it's your future you're discussing, your judgement can get a little foggy. This is not a time for self-indulgence. Continue to put the company's needs first. Describe how you will solve their problems and add value. Be "them-oriented" not "me-oriented." Remember, there are two reasons why people are hired: to solve a problem and to add value.

The more you can demonstrate how your past efforts made a difference, and how the same talents and skills will make a difference with the new company, the better position you have at the negotiating table. You must make this value apparent to the hiring authority. The more you can convince them of your worth, the better your negotiating stance.

By making the negotiation process one of understanding each other's needs, and identifying options and alternatives to best meet those needs, you and the hiring authority will keep the negotiations agreeable. You should stay in a determined, yet flexible, state of mind. Remain pleasant, reasonable, and assertive. (Not aggressive. There is a great expanse between passivity and aggressiveness—that is assertiveness.)

❑ Avoid unreasonable demands.

❑ Refrain from making minor issues major hang-ups.

❑ Stay away from emotional terms or reactions:

"That's crazy."

"Here we go again. Another low ball offer."

"I can't believe with all of my experience, this is the offer you're presenting."

❑ Think positively about what you can achieve by negotiating, and be prepared.

◈ Getting Paid What You're Worth ◈

The very first step in negotiating a salary is to be well prepared. If your only preparation is a list of demands, including a minimum dollar amount which you want, you will be doomed. The better prepared you are prior to the interview, the more confidence you will have, and the better salary you will negotiate.

◈ Know What You Have To Offer ◈

You know your skills and talents (see exercises in Part One). Before going to an interview, identify the skills and talents which you enjoy using most—which will benefit this company. How will your skills help the company? This is not a time for modesty. This is a time to sell yourself. What makes you unique? What do you do so well that this employer needs you? How can you:

❑ improve productivity?

❑ create better morale?

❑ service their customers better?

❑ cut their operation costs?

❑ increase quality?

❑ create better products?

❑ manage better?

❑ sell better?

In essence, how can you contribute more than you will cost the employer? When you identify and communicate your worth to the employer during the interview, you will have a much better chance of reaching a mutually-agreeable salary.

✌ Your Interests ✌

Your career values are guideposts to follow during negotiations. Because you know what you want, you can focus in that direction. Everything you say brings you closer to your goal. The clearer you are about your interests, the more likely you are to have them met.

Remember, your career values are truly important to your job satisfaction—and your personal happiness. They will make your job seem like play.

Each party at a negotiating table has their own agenda. If you are clear about what you want—based on your value to the company—you won't have to become emotional. You'll be able to talk about issues and facts, which will lead to a mutually-satisfying offer.

✌ Their Interests ✌

The better you understand the employer's interests, the easier it will be to develop options and alternatives. You will need to ask questions—before and during the interview. Don't guess or make assumptions.

Try to put yourself in their place. What motivates them to feel as they do? Again, talk to their vendors, customers, and previous and current employees. Ask questions such as:

❑ What is their reputation?

❑ How do they treat their employees?

❑ Are they known to have average, above average, or below average compensation packages?

❑ What types of benefits do they offer?

❑ What do you like about the company?

❑ What areas do you think need improvement?

Also, discover what you can about the hiring authority. What type of reputation do they have? You might try to talk with someone who currently works for the hiring authority. (They probably negotiated their salary.) What suggestions can they give you? Talk with someone who used to work for the hiring authority. What advice do they have for you?

If you can't acquire much information on the company or the hiring authority prior to the interview, ask permission to talk with some of the employees who will be your co-workers. Ask these employees about the company and the hiring authority. Try to acquire an understanding of the company's and the department's needs and concerns. Seek the employees' advice on salary issues. Is the company rigid or flexible? (Although talking with current employees is an excellent way to obtain information on the company, you must use discretion. You can't be sure what role any one individual might have in the final hiring decision.)

Even though you might have been successful in obtaining a lot of information from the above sources, in order to fully understand the hiring authority's point of view, you must ask them questions during the interview. You must understand their interests and expectations. Also, to determine if this is the right job for you, you will need to ask the hiring authority about:

❑ Your responsibilities: what is expected of you.

❑ The lines of command: who you will report to.

❑ Problems that need solving: both department and company-wide.

❑ Your potential for professional growth.

❑ The company's financial position/stability.

❑ An expected salary range.

> Negotiating the best deal is not an event which happens at the end of an interview; it is a process which can begin long before an interview occurs.

You should phrase questions in such a way that the hiring authority feels you are asking for their advice (remember, people love to give advice): "What do you think the major problems are?", "Do you have any ideas on what could be done?", "How receptive is management?", or "How long do you think it will take to make changes?"

When you ask for their advice, you are demonstrating that you respect their opinion. This makes the hiring authority feel good.

Be aware of your facial reactions and the tone of your voice. Sometimes what you say is not as important as how you say it. Keep in mind, this is not a win or lose situation. The better you both understand each other, the more satisfying the outcome of the negotiations.

As you ask questions, your main goal is to make the hiring authority feel heard and understood. Listen with your whole body. Use eye contact and body language which shows you are paying attention. Avoid listening only to what you want to hear: selective hearing. Instead, hear what the hiring authority is trying to communicate. You must listen without attaching your personal beliefs to what is being said. You must listen without thinking about how you will respond.

When you listen, you don't have to agree with what the hiring authority says. You only have to accept the fact that they feel the way they feel or that they want what they say they want. At this stage, don't try to counter what they say, simply listen and be sensitive to their beliefs.

This may take some practice. Usually we expect others to view the world as we do. Understanding your potential employer's interests is imperative to reaching an agreement. As you listen to the hiring authority, ask "why" and "what": "Why do you suggest doing it that way?", "What is the purpose of the new product?", or "What will help me better understand your concerns?"

When you respect their position you will have a much better chance of seeing positive results from your negotiating. You will be able to orient your side of the discussion to best appeal to their interests and beliefs. To make the hiring authority feel understood, paraphrase what they say. Remember, the purpose of negotiating is to meet both their needs and yours.

❧ How To Get The Most Money ❧

Once you understand the employer's wants, you can begin interjecting your needs into the discussion. Never forget that your primary purpose at the early stage of the interview is to communicate how you will add value. When you address the employer's needs first, you are actually building your worth in their eyes—and that is a big part of negotiating. The more value you are to them, the more compensation they will be willing to give you in return.

The single most effective way to establish your value is to give examples of problems you solved and solutions you created. Provide details of what you have achieved and what skills you have to offer. Facts and figures increase your credibility. Explain how your accomplishments relate to their needs. Give as many reasons as possible for them to want you. In today's competitive market you must demonstrate not just that you can fit, but that you stand out.

Maybe their initial offer is acceptable to you. If that's the case, express enthusiasm, ask for a written confirmation, and indicate you will be in touch very shortly, to make sure everything is progressing.

However, seldom are things quite that easy. Most likely you will need to negotiate. Be wary of trying to "start off on the right foot" with a new employer by accepting whatever salary they offer you. Don't give up on *your* goals. No one will withdraw an offer because you feel you're worth more. And, by wanting to negotiate, you might even increase your value to them. It might show that you are willing to discuss issues that are important to you, rather than just accepting other peoples' views.

You are at the pinnacle of negotiating leverage when you've received an offer. Thus, if the salary or benefit package is not to your liking, realize your bargaining power is good. Usually, employers have some latitude and are able to adjust the offer—but don't appear too greedy. Be careful in making demands which you might regret later. Don't let salary be the sole issue. It is only one aspect of a career position. Continue to balance your desires with the employer's needs. Other factors to consider include:

- ❑ Is this job something you really want to do?
- ❑ Do you like the company?
- ❑ Does the potential career progression fulfill your goals?
- ❑ Is the salary in line with the responsibilities?
- ❑ Do you like the location of the company?
- ❑ Does the benefit package meet your needs?
- ❑ Is your boss someone with whom you could work?
- ❑ Can you get along with the other co-workers?

⛋ Salary ⛋

The first time you think about salary should not be during the negotiation stage of the interview. Instead, you must conduct some research before the interview to determine the general salary range for the job. Some positions have a salary which is cast in stone. Other salaries are negotiable. You need to know if yours is. If it is negotiable, you need to determine what other people are paid to do a similar job. There are several ways to do this. One is to discover the pay levels for similar positions, at companies that are about the same size, in the same industry.

Another way is to contact the human resources department at the potential employer, and ask what the range is for the available position. A third option is to use any of the following sources:

- ❏ Employment Agencies
- ❏ Executive Search Firms
- ❏ Salary Surveys
- ❏ Professional Associations
- ❏ Jobs Rated Almanac
- ❏ Occupational Outlook Handbook
- ❏ American Almanac of Jobs and Salaries
- ❏ American Salaries and Wages Survey
- ❏ *Employment and Earnings* (U.S. Department of Labor)

What should you do if the topic of salary comes up before you've had time to establish your worth? You can say: "Salary won't be a problem. Can we first talk about how we might benefit each other, and come back to salary a little later?" or "I sure want to talk about salary at some point but I'm not clear on several other issues. Can I ask a few more questions, and then we can get back to salary?"

Once the hiring authority has decided that you are the right person for the position, it's okay to talk about compensation, but not before.

The hiring authority might introduce the subject like this, "We've had a great visit today. I think you'd be perfect for the position. What kind of money did you have in mind?"

Beware: do not trap yourself by answering this question. **You should not be the first person to mention a salary amount.** If you do, you could hurt yourself in one of two ways. If you state a salary level which is too high, it could scare the employer off and they won't make you an offer. They assume you won't be satisfied. If you state a figure that is too low, you could lose out on some potential income.

How should you respond to a question like that? There are several approaches you can use, however, always remember to reemphasize your interest in the position and how you can contribute to the company: "Salary is not my most important priority. I'm much more interested in being able to contribute...to feel as though I'm making a difference...in getting established with a company that is growing and that will appreciate what I can offer."

Then you can throw the ball back in their court by adding: "Since salary isn't my most important priority, why don't you make me an offer—which you feel is fair for what I can do for you. Let's start from there."

The employer may throw out a number and say: "Well, we were planning to offer somewhere around $50,000. How do you feel about that?" or they may play the game a little longer by saying: "I understand what you're saying but everyone has a figure in mind. What's yours?"

Don't give in yet. You don't want to back down at crucial moments, and this may be one of them. On the other hand, you don't want to antagonize the hiring authority. Be patient. Maybe you can let a few moments of silence work for you. Also, show that you are sensitive to the employer's line of thinking: "Bill, I know you're just trying to get some direction. Let me reiterate one more time, salary is not my most important priority. However I'm accustomed to earning in the $45,000 to $55,000 range. And it is human nature that we all like to grow both professionally, as well as monetarily, so do the best you can, and I'll contribute for all I'm worth."

Most likely, the employer will stop pressing, and offer a dollar amount.

Another way to avoid naming a specific figure first is to go through the scenario of what you will contribute, and salary not being your most important issue, then ask: "What did you have in mind for someone with my skills and talents?" or "If you had the perfect person for this job, what would you ideally pay them?" or "Can you tell me what the salary range for the position is?"

Any of those questions should get you to the point of a specific figure. Remember the basic premise is to keep both parties' interests in mind, so you can arrive at a mutually-satisfying agreement. At this point, the hiring authority is probably anxious to hire you so they want to cooperate as much as possible. However, their thoughts are focused on how much money it will take before you accept the offer, and how they can offer you that amount without disturbing the internal salary structure of the company.

Oftentimes you will be asked to state your current salary. Try to stay away from being judged by your salary history. Be judged on your value to the potential employer. What you were last paid doesn't necessarily prove your worth to a new employer.

If you are asked what your last salary was, you can answer by explaining that your last compensation package was based on a completely different set of priorities. Point out how the two positions differ, and use the opportunity to again express your value in terms of what you expect to accomplish for the new employer. Also, if you can come up with a dollar amount or percentage figure for the value your talents will add, your previous salary has less significance.

Once a salary has been offered, you are ready for the next step. If the figure is not what you expected, you might be able to use silence to your benefit. Many times, silence on your part will lead the hiring authority to offer more. If silence doesn't work, and a higher figure is not offered, reiterate your views. Let the potential employer know you understand their needs. Talk again about your interests, based on the value you will add to the company. If there is still no change in the offer, try to discover what other factors might be affecting the salary amount. "Where does this figure fit in the salary range for this position?" (Most large companies prefer to make offers at or below the middle point.) "How does this salary compare with what other employees who are adding similar value are receiving?" (If the salary research you did is applicable, you could discuss it now.)

If you sense the hiring authority is getting uncomfortable, back off. Begin to discuss alternatives. You can always return to the issue of money later. Sometimes the hiring authority wants more time to think about what you've said or they need approval from others in the company before they can make changes to the original offer. In other words, sometimes you won't be able to leave the interview with a firm salary offer. The hiring authority might say: "Ken, I have a good understanding of what you're looking for. I'd like to talk with a few other people here, to see what we can come up with. How about if I get back to you in a couple of days?"

Indicate that this would be fine. But before you leave, once again express your enthusiasm for the job and state how you are anxious to contribute to the company. Demonstrate confidence that the compensation situation will work itself out.

Remember, salary is only one component of compensation.

↳ Other Perks To Consider ↲

You can't establish an agreement which is fair to both the employer and yourself without considering options and alternatives. I discussed salary first, because it is often so important to people. But by discussing alternative perks, you will reach the best agreement for both of you. Let's examine what other options might be available. What else can go into your compensation package? Here are some of the possibilities:

❏ dental insurance	❏ pay for performance	❏ life insurance
❏ medical insurance	❏ bonuses	❏ auto insurance
❏ disability insurance	❏ profit sharing	❏ vision insurance
❏ 401K plans	❏ pension benefits	❏ personal leave
❏ illness leave	❏ investment matching	❏ job sharing
❏ group discounts	❏ tuition reimbursement	❏ company car
❏ child care	❏ family counseling	❏ car allowance
❏ flexible hours	❏ personal business days	❏ stock options
❏ relocation expenses	❏ association dues	❏ legal services
❏ floating holidays	❏ vacation time	❏ mileage

In addition to a base salary, the employer may offer some or all of these perks. Sometimes employers have a cafeteria-style compensation package available, where you can pick and choose from a selection of optional perks. The idea is to develop choices and to agree on a compensation package which best meets your needs. Brainstorm together. If you don't need some of the perks that are offered, make trade-offs.

The more you discuss your compensation package, the better deal you will receive. Additionally, you will have conveyed that you are truly trying to cooperate with the employer in reaching a fair compensation package. Don't concentrate too much on money or any other single aspect. You don't want to lose sight of different ways to make the agreement work. Ask for cooperation: "What do you think about____?" If you get stuck on a small detail move it aside and go onto something else. Keep the atmosphere friendly.

Constantly consider the employer's interests—and mention them—while at the same time keeping your goals in mind. Muster all of the energy you can, but don't be aggressive and try to take control. Keep reminding yourself how compensation negotiations are best accomplished:

Your Interests—Their Interests

Open and Honest Communication

Options—Alternatives

Different Packages—Best for Both Parties

Be patient. Many beneficial changes can come your way by being patient. Disappointments typically come from a lack of patience.

✌ Salary Alternatives ☙

If the discussion is going well, yet salary is still an unsolved issue, there are alternative agreements for you to consider:

❑   A sign-on bonus. (This won't affect any internal equity situation, yet it will give you what you feel you're worth.)

❑   Request a performance and salary review after three or six months, instead of the standard one-year period.

❑ A pay for performance option. (Either a stock option incentive or a percentage of salary contingent on performance.)

❑ A year-end bonus if certain conditions are met.

❑ A title change to a higher grade, creating greater salary flexibility.

❑ Take on additional duties, thereby allowing a salary increase for the added responsibility.

If you diligently follow these suggestions, you will usually reach a mutually-beneficial agreement. Sometimes, this might not happen in one sitting. Don't get disappointed and don't give up hope.

> The idea is to develop choices and to agree on a compensation package which best meets your needs.

Negotiating The Job

Too many people assume that to earn as much as possible, they must do work they don't like. Material goods will not bring you satisfaction. Only by doing what you believe is right and by making a difference for others will you find the satisfaction and success you deserve.

One option you should always consider is knowing when it is time to walk away. That's right. It might be time to walk away from a job offer if:

❑ You feel in your heart this job isn't right for you.

❑ You decide you cannot make a difference.

❑ The hiring authority pays no attention to your reasonable requests.

❑ Your career values are not being met.

❑ Repeated attempts to reach an agreement are all one-sided.

Not every job opportunity will be the right one for you. If this one isn't, there will be one that is.

The more a job utilizes your skills and meets your career values, the better it will ultimately be for you. Keep this in mind as you negotiate your job. You might want to bargain for specific responsibilities which suit who you are and what you do best.

Once you've accepted a job offer, your next goal should be to accomplish what you said you would for the company. Also, don't get so wrapped up in your new job that you lose sight of the continuing negotiations which prove your worth and value to the company. Your return on these daily efforts can be phenomenal. I call them, "negotiating on the inside."

❧ Receive A Better Raise, Sooner ❧

Inside negotiating is ongoing. It requires frequent and honest communication. As you and your boss work together to determine goals, chart progress, and plan for rewards, the annual performance review of the past becomes a much less formal occurrence. Each meeting with your manager should be used to brainstorm ideas, comment on successes, and suggest improvements.

At your earliest opportunity, determine what is important to your boss and the company. Don't assume you know what other people desire. Try to view the world as your boss does. What do they mean by what they say or do? Discuss their values—and yours.

If you follow these suggestions, you will be an outstanding employee, and you'll receive a better raise, sooner:

❏ Learn why you were hired.

❏ Establish goals and constantly monitor your progress. Make sure you know what is expected of you; and then do more.

❏ See the good in others. Avoid criticizing.

❏ Communicate a little better each day.

❑ Practice self improvement, wrapped around a daily pursuit of perfection. Your improvement will come gradually, but over time it will add up to a significant competitive advantage.

❑ Be a problem solver, not just a problem identifier. Always have a project and a goal you are working on. After all, that is one of the reasons you were hired: to solve problems.

❑ Resist the tendency to look to others for solutions. Empower yourself. Let solutions start with you.

❑ Constantly try to make things better. Don't just work hard, make sure you are also adding value.

❑ Please all internal and external customers. A good way to maintain this focus is to think like a business owner. When you feel completely responsible for your part of the company, you will have greater flexibility to do your job as you really want to do it. You'll be more involved with the products or services, the customers, the problems, and the solutions. You won't feel so confined by a narrow routine. You'll plan for the future and you'll know what you want to achieve in the next six months or the next year. You'll have a better concept of where the company is going, and what your role is in helping them get there.

❑ Always think strategically and plan your actions.

❑ Develop relationships (rapport) with people throughout the entire company.

❑ Embrace change and display an upbeat, positive attitude of enthusiasm and energy.

❑ Have a sense of humor.

↙ Being Appreciated ↘

Because you are doing a great job does not necessarily mean it is obvious to those in authority. You need to paint a detailed picture of how your contributions are benefiting the organization and your boss. This is the second phase of negotiating on the inside. Others, particularly management, must recognize and appreciate your efforts. Remember, your boss' primary concern is how your performance reflects on them.

Demonstrate how your actions are adding value to one or more of the three primary areas of business concern: increasing profits, saving time or money, and improving customer satisfaction. You can add value to any one of these areas through:

❑ New Technology
❑ Improved Organization
❑ Greater Productivity
❑ Creative Ideas
❑ Improved Relationships

❑ Better People Management
❑ Increased Morale
❑ Better Quality
❑ Implementing Changes
❑ Time Management

When a boss perceives that your contributions are helping them succeed or that you are removing burdens and making their job easier, your efforts will be noticed. When you are viewed favorably and your performance exceeds expectations, you will directly benefit. Thus, it is important for you to keep your accomplishments in the open.

Keep an accomplishment diary. Write a paragraph every time you complete a task. It doesn't have to be a huge accomplishment. Write down anything that benefits the company and makes you feel proud.

Communicate often with your boss. Continuously show your boss how you are adding value. (Be aware of how much of your boss' time you take: don't make them regret seeing you at their door.) A way to avoid being a pest is to turn your boss into a mentor. Make them feel proud that they are contributing to your growth, while the company also benefits from your performance.

If your efforts make your boss look good, your boss will have a genuine interest in your success. Ask for their advice on your ideas and methods. And, occasionally, ask your boss for an honest, off-the-cuff appraisal of your performance. See if there is more you can do to better serve the department or the company. Discuss the quality of your work and the satisfaction level of your customers. This will emphasize that you are a dedicated, results-oriented individual.

If you communicate these issues on a regular basis, your value is maintained and probably even increased in your boss' eyes. When the time comes, your boss will find it much easier to reward you.

No matter how well you think you are performing, keep in mind you are not automatically entitled to salary increases and promotions. Do not rest on your laurels. Develop new skills. Take on new responsibilities. Your individual growth and the promotions you receive will increase your compensation.

Keep updated on salary levels and perks for the job you are doing. Stay in touch with professional associations and other sources which can provide this information.

These strategies for negotiating on the inside will accelerate your development and compound your return on compensation throughout your career. Practice them daily. You will greatly benefit from it.

In Review

Many employers feel that job candidates who negotiate professionally during an interview are treated with greater respect and offered more opportunities. From day one, you are positioning for your future value, which can mean a difference of thousands of dollars over the course of your career.

You have learned that cooperative negotiation eliminates anger, frustration, disappointment, and the feeling of being taken advantage of. It will bring you a high level of self-esteem, job satisfaction, life balance, and inner peace—which is what you are seeking.

After reading all of this material, are you beginning to doubt if you want to work for someone else? Is your intuition telling you that you should start a business and be your own boss? If so, you'll want to read the next chapter, where I'll discuss what it takes to be an entrepreneur, and you'll be able to decide if owning a business is the right thing for you.

Part Five

Unleashing
Your Passion

14

Being Your Own Boss

More than seventy-five percent of the work force want to quit their jobs and start their own businesses. Most won't try. Some will—and will fail. Others will work their fingers to the bone—and just get by. A small percentage will have mediocre success. And a few will hit the jackpot—but not because they were lucky. The few who succeed at being their own boss were prepared to run their own business *before* they started it.

There is enough information on how to start and run a profitable business venture to fill a library. You can read booklets, pamphlets, magazines, and books. You can listen to tapes and watch videos. You can even attend seminars. But if you aren't able to be your own boss, none of this information will help you succeed. Let's face it, not everyone has what it takes to be an entrepreneur. It's not in everyone's makeup. So, before you begin researching how to start your own business, and surely before you begin investing any money in a venture, first determine if you *really* want to start your own business:

- ❑ Do you have the skills, traits, and personality required to run your own business?
- ❑ Is it worth the financial and emotional risks?
- ❑ Are you willing to put forth a lot of effort?
- ❑ Will you be able to find a business that suits you?
- ❑ Is the timing right?
- ❑ Do you have your family's support?
- ❑ What if it doesn't work?

Whether or not to own a business is a tough decision and it is not one to make quickly or lightly. Since I've been through this decision making process myself, and I've helped thousands of others successfully reach a decision, I can help you too. There are ways to substantially reduce the risk involved in starting your own venture, buying a business, or getting involved with a franchise. The first is knowing if you are right for the job.

Far too many small businesses fail because the owner is not prepared emotionally or financially. With an eighty percent failure rate within the first three years, it is imperative that you think it through before making such a change in your life.

Luckily, with the guidance in this chapter, it can be rather simple for you to begin reaching some conclusions. And, when you have some answers, you and your family can feel more confident about the decision you make.

Maybe you've dreamt of owning your own business for a long time or maybe it's a new idea. Maybe you feel you have no choice, as the result of too many lay offs or a lack of available jobs in your area. Maybe you hate your job and you just don't want to work for anyone else again. Any of these reasons could be causing you to think about being your own boss. Some are valid, some are not. I'll tell you why, and the importance of knowing the difference.

How Change Can Benefit You

It is imperative to look at change and to understand it. If you view change incorrectly or you let change hamper your decision making abilities, you might reach conclusions you end up regretting.

People change jobs. Jobs change. Careers come and go. What is new today is that change is happening faster than ever before. In the last several years, over fifty percent of our country's companies were restructured. One hundred thousand organizations were either acquired or merged. Companies have changed their product lines and cut their design cycles. New markets have been forged. Businesses were relocated. Budgets were cut and jobs were slashed.

Over the last forty years, the percentage of employees involved in manufacturing dropped from seventy-three percent to less than fifteen percent. Technology, an expanding and more competitive global economy, cost cutting, and forced work reductions all add to the vast changes in how and why we work.

We are in the Information Age. Services and knowledge will lead the way. Two-thirds of the work force will be involved in service of some kind—with knowledge (expertise) being the most important product.

While Fortune 500 companies have lost over three million jobs, small- and medium-sized companies are growing and creating new opportunities. Companies with fewer than twenty employees will be responsible for more than half of the new jobs within this decade. Firms with twenty to fifty employees will create another third of the new opportunities.

Because of the rapid pace of change in the business world, more and more people are considering work alternatives. Forty-five million people do all or at least a part of their job from their homes. There are thirteen million self-employed people who work at home.

Over the years, a large percentage of the work force grew accustomed to a certain amount of job security. Careers followed a pattern of growth. As you worked hard and gained experience, new opportunities were presented. Promotions were offered; you did not have to necessarily seek them out. Sure, there was always office politics, but even the politics created opportunities, which in turn brought growth for individuals. Now that type of growth is much more limited. Companies are leaner. There is not as much people movement, thus, many of those growth opportunities no longer exist.

The corporate ladder is quickly losing its rungs. With fewer growth positions available, and more and more college graduates competing for those opportunities, growth via promotions has drastically decreased. A career path which existed before is now overgrown. There isn't a clear route.

No longer does the traditional concept of a lifelong job with benefits exist. (College graduates entering the work force today are expected to have twelve different jobs and three different careers!) You will be hard pressed to find: a lifetime job, job security, a corporate ladder to climb, or a career path to follow, or one lifetime career. Typically, employment is treated on a "project" basis: after the project is completed, your services might not be required any more.

The burden of responsibility for career growth is no longer on the employer. Your employer will not protect your future. Corporations no longer owe you continued employment, promotions, or regular salary increases.

Actuarial tables show that people are living longer. With this longer life expectancy comes better health and a financial need to work later in life. If you are going to work longer, it makes sense to do something which fits your talents and interests. So again, thoughts of controlling your destiny by being your own boss come to the forefront.

Every year, more and more people join the ranks of the self-employed. Entrepreneurs are coming from two age groups: those between twenty-five and thirty-five years of age, and those between fifty and sixty years of age. (Women and minorities are also adding to the trend. They are venturing into the retail and service industries for niche markets, which is where the major growth is occurring.)

You must adapt to these changes—the question is "How?"

Stress

Many workers, both blue and white collar, are worn down by the pace of change. Depression and insomnia have escalated. Stress poses a documented danger to our overall health. Acute levels of stress lead to migraine headaches and heart disease. In fact, as many as eighty to ninety percent of the maladies seen by doctors are caused by stress.

It's no wonder people are seeking relief from the stress by taking control of their lives. In a recent poll conducted by *U.S. News and World Report*, fifty percent of the survey respondents said they had recently taken steps to simplify their lives. People are moving to smaller communities, decreasing their work hours, and turning down promotions in favor of less stress. They want more time for themselves, even if it means less money. They are seeking a better balance in their lives.

When asked to identify what was important to them, the survey participants ranked their lives like this:

1. Family Life
2. Spiritual Life
3. Health
4. Financial Situation
5. Job
6. Romantic Life
7. Leisure Time
8. Home

How are you doing in these categories? The survey participants said they were doing fairly well in all but three categories: their financial situations, their jobs, and their leisure time. (Notice all three are career related!)

The two biggest factors which contribute to a person's quality of life are: family relationships and job/career satisfaction. When you work in the right job, both of these factors are usually satisfied.

Which brings us back to the question of owning a business. Is entrepreneurship for you? Will you be able to attain a higher level of satisfaction by being your own boss? Too often when you become dissatisfied with your job, your first assumption is, "I'll only be happy when I'm my own boss." There is far too much at stake—your life—to make such a hasty supposition without the basis of research.

Making Work Fun

In order to be a successful business owner, you must live your job. In fact, there should be little distinction between work and play. Both should bring you similar levels of satisfaction.

Will owning a business give you what you want from life? Will it give you a reason to get out of bed each morning? Remember all of the work you did on self discovery in the first part of this book? You'll use a lot of that information as you contemplate becoming an entrepreneur.

Happiness comes from within. It's not about things. It's about who you are, what you enjoy doing, and how you can make a difference in other people's lives. Be who you are—follow your heart, using the talents and skills you enjoy using, in circumstances where your values are met. Your satisfaction will come from using your uniqueness every day, to make a difference in the world. It won't come from material possessions.

When who you are comes across in your daily activities, you will have found your passion. And the feelings you will experience are worth the time it will take to discover the right job. It is good that you are at least considering entrepreneurship as a possibility to job happiness. All things should be considered when trying to attain a balance in your life.

If you don't take the chance to live your life the way you want to live it, you may never know your true worth.

If you're going to succeed as an entrepreneur, you'll have to adopt the philosophy that your work and life will become one.

Why Consider Entrepreneurship?

The allure of doing your own thing appeals to the masses. But what makes this way of earning a living so enticing? Why do seventy-five percent of people think owning a business is the road to happiness? What are some of the *negative* life events which prompt people to think about starting a business of their own?   Following are the most frequently stated reasons people give for starting their own business:

1. **You're not being paid what you're worth.** You feel trapped in a corporate salary range. Your boss doesn't appreciate what you do for the company. When a salary and performance review occurs, the company's guidelines must be followed, and a four percent increase doesn't offer much. Overall, the company's attitude is, "You should be glad you have a job."

2. **Your talents are under-utilized.** You are in a rut and dissatisfied. In fact, you hate your job.

3. **There is no opportunity for advancement or growth.** Although you are doing a great job for the company, there is no movement in the ranks above you. The ladder of progression is full and it could be years before someone leaves, retires, or dies.

4. **You're in a depressed industry.** In your industry the activity is in cutbacks. Morale is low and the general atmosphere is quite depressing.

5. **You're not allowed to make decisions.** Although you are very capable, management insists on maintaining the status quo: three levels of approval before any changes are made.

6. **You are forced into early retirement.** You were looking forward to retirement—ten years from now—not today. You still need (and want) to work.

7. **You've been re-engineered, again.** For the third time in your career, you've been affected by a company-wide reduction. It's nothing against you or your performance on the job—it's just the economy. You feel as though you have no control over your career.

Do any of these sound familiar? One is no more valid than another, and all of them give people reasons to believe there must be a better way.

Are there wrong reasons for wanting to own a business? Yes. Following are eight inappropriate reasons for wanting to be an entrepreneur:

1. **You're *slightly* dissatisfied with your job.** To be successful in your own business, you must have a passion to do it. You will have to eat, live, and breathe the business, at least for awhile. A temporary dissatisfaction with your current job does not produce a passion.

2. **You want to get rich.** If you're setting out to earn your fortune, consider this: most schemes to earn a lot of money quickly and easily don't work. With the right personality, skills, and attitude; and the right business idea, you might arrive at a fortune. But that is different than starting your own business to become a millionaire. If your business succeeds because you have a unique product or service to provide, that's great. But a desire for money hasn't kept anyone happy in their job.

3. **You're having problems communicating with your boss and you feel you could do better.** There are many risks involved in business ownership. Be sure your problem at work isn't temporary before you make major life changes.

4. **You want to set your own work hours and have lots of leisure time.** The commitment to establish and maintain your own busi-

ness will probably take more time and energy than you ever antici-pated. Don't be fooled by this type of wishful thinking.

5. **You need a job—or you don't like your current job.** Business ownership is much more than a job. It is a way of life and it takes a huge level of commitment.

6. **You want to prove to your previous employer that you shouldn't have been laid off.** Any action taken because of anger or a grudge will most likely backfire. The drive to start a business must come from a passion, not an external whim.

7. **You want less stress in your life.** If stress easily affects you nega-tively, you should talk with some entrepreneurs. Find out what it was like for them when they first started their businesses. You might end up increasing your stress, with longer work hours and tighter finances.

8. **You're tired of looking for a job.** Even if you can't bear the thought of another rejection, you need lots more than a failing job search to propel you into business ownership. You need to enter entrepre-neurship with enthusiasm and passion, not with tired feet and low self-esteem.

If any of the above reasons are why you're considering starting a business, learn more about entrepreneurship before you proceed fur-ther. Weigh the risks against the rewards. Know what to expect. It might help to consider the pros and the cons of business ownership.

The Pros of Being Your Own Boss

1. Self-Esteem

For many people, there is a certain amount of glamour involved in own-ing a business. They feel proud when they say, "I work for me. I'm my own boss. I have my own business."

2. Personal Growth

When you are responsible for a business, you are involved in so many facets that you automatically grow as a person. You'll encounter responsibilities you've never had before: finances, taxes, accounting, regulations, budgeting, employee relations, pricing, advertising, purchasing, etc. Your true talents will blossom and achievements will be made.

3. Independence and Control

When you are the boss, you make all the decisions. You choose where to work, and with whom. You are in control of your future. You face no risk of a layoff, mandatory retirement, or being fired. You have created your job security.

4. Flexibility

You can use your skills and talents in a variety of ways. People change their minds about what they want to do. As an employee, you might be confined to using certain skills. As your own boss, you can choose which skills to use.

5. Financial Advantages

Your own business can offer tax advantages you never realized as an employee. And if your venture is successful, you have the possibility of increasing your financial worth.

6. Family Advantages

Family members can benefit from your business. They could work in the business, learn new skills, and grow to new heights.

As you contemplate these positive elements of owning a business, think about what you have learned over the years. Is there any one particular aspect of your experience that you really enjoyed? Can you improve upon that or do it better than it's being done now? Could you show others how to do it better? Remember, we are in an age when knowledge is a commodity.

If you already have an idea about what type of business you'd like to start, imagine various parts of the business. Picture yourself going about the daily activity of running it. How does it make you feel? Is there any one aspect which excites you more than others? This mental exercise can provide clues regarding particular advantages which are meaningful to you.

The Cons of Being Your Own Boss

1. Risk

The odds are not in favor of new small business ventures. If your business failed, could you handle it? What stigmas do you attach to failure? How long would it take you to recover—emotionally and financially? What would you do next? Did you invest most (all?) of your personal savings into the venture? Did you put a lien on your home? A business failure will mean more debt. Could you stand it? What would it do to your family? What if your relatives or friends loaned money towards your business? Could they handle the financial loss?

And in today's society, business owners face many legal risks, from employees, customers, and product liability. Is all of this stress worth it?

2. Responsibility

Greater responsibility can help you grow—or you might realize you are not ready for so many new duties. You might never have had to do so many things before. You're not good at making decisions, and you're beginning to make mistakes. There is a lot of stress involved in not doing things well. There is a lot of uncertainty, and not much return in all of this responsibility. Can you handle the stress?

3. Big Change

You are getting into something brand new. You're leaving the familiar behind to face the unknown. Maybe for most of your career, you chose safety over risk. How will you fare in this new game, with its own rules? Can you operate without a corporate shield that wielded both power and company perks?

4. Financial

There is always plenty at stake in a new business, especially if you have risked your savings. In addition to whatever capital it required to start the business, you could need lots more to keep it going. You don't want cash flow to doom your venture. It could take years for the business to turn a profit. Can you wait that long?

5. Family and Friends

If your family and friends support your venture, they can provide a tremendous boost and help you over some rough spots. However, if they don't share your enthusiasm or your vision of success, their lack of support can be a roadblock to your progress. Negative comments from family and friends can take a toll, eventually causing you so much stress that your business fails.

Why Businesses Fail

I don't like to use the word "fail." I much prefer taking planned actions, getting results, analyzing the results, and altering actions until the desired results are realized. However, if you are deciding whether or not to start a business, you must acknowledge the fact that not everyone has the staying power to achieve what they think they want. Therefore, I would be remiss if I didn't discuss documented reasons why entrepreneurs don't reach their goals:

1. **Lack of preparation.** Many would-be entrepreneurs never even take the time to do what you are doing right now: trying to determine if they are well-suited to being their own boss. As you well know, this is only the first step in a long examination of the many facets of business ownership. As a result of this lack of preparation, people get into the wrong business or they create the wrong organizational structure, which has legal, tax, and financial ramifications.

2. **Unrealistic expectations.** This could be a result of poor prepara-

tion or it may be a case of wearing rose-colored glasses. Sometimes the thrill and excitement of a new venture clouds even the most sensible person. You might be so anxious to get the doors open that you let eternal optimism rule your thinking. Maybe you've projected sales or income which don't have a prayer of coming to fruition. And, if you've also fooled yourself about the risk tolerance of your life-style expectations, you could become depressed and frustrated rather quickly.

3. Lack of market potential. Research and analysis into the viability of a product or service is imperative. You can't project market potential on your thoughts only. Markets change quickly, and no one business will ever dictate what a market will buy. The market tells businesses what it wants, and under what circumstances it will buy it. If your market never develops, it could be because you've targeted the wrong segment or niche of the market.

4. Unexpected competition. You must know your competition inside out. Too many people anticipate or presume who their competition is, and don't study the market. Maybe the competition is planning to do it better or cheaper than you can do it. Or your entry into the marketplace may cause jealousy, stirring the competition to action, causing price wars or improved products. You must be ready to counter; yet you can't concentrate so much effort on your competition that you forget your customers.

5. Poor financial management. If you are not talented in financial management, get some help. Maybe you didn't have enough capital from the start, or maybe you underestimated your needs. Did you spend too much on assets, too soon? Are your credit terms for your customers too liberal? Either of these mistakes could result in severe cash flow problems. If the finances get away from you, your business may never recover.

6. Too accustomed to being an employee. Many people can learn to be entrepreneurs, though some people fear or resist change too much and it just won't happen. If you are too accustomed to a structured working environment, it could be too difficult for you to take on the challenge of being your own boss.

Maybe you rely on the support you receive as an employee—you don't want to do all of the menial tasks yourself. You're used to performing your job in a certain way, and you don't want to change. That's fine, as long as you realize it now, and know you can be happy as an employee. Don't force entrepreneurship upon yourself. Many try to force it and end up failing.

7. Poor marketing. Marketing is a science. For any business, it is as critical as proper financial management. You can't expect to hang out your shingle and have customers walk through your door. You must figure out a precise formula to attract customers. If you develop an ineffective marketing plan (or have none at all) you will be in trouble. Your advertising must produce results and your sales techniques must be up-to-date and customer-oriented.

8. Growth. No, this isn't in the wrong category. Sometimes growth happens too quickly, and your financial and people assets are stretched to the breaking point. You could then face additional problems. Product or service quality may decline. Employee morale can sour, affecting customer service. You must manage growth, just as you do other aspects of your business.

9. Unexpected disasters. A disaster could be a new invention or product which drives you out of business. Or the economy could change, making times lean for you. And, sometimes disaster comes from Mother Nature: hurricanes, floods, fire, etc.

10. Poor management. I didn't place this at the end of the list because it occurs less often than the others, rather because the other nine are probably influenced by poor management, too. Owning and managing a business is an all-encompassing job. You need leadership, communication, marketing, and financial skills in addition to lots of stamina.

The generic term, "poor management" can be summed up by saying that ninety percent of business failures are usually caused by poor planning, bad decisions, poor business sense, or a general lack of experience. The key is to seek advice from experts in the areas where you need help.

If your interest to start a business is still strong, you must now make sure that your talents and values lend themselves to owning a business.

Do You Have What It Takes?

Maybe running your own business will finally put you in your niche. It gets you to the top of the pyramid, where twenty percent of people who truly enjoy their work reside. If your skills are biased towards owning a business, it may be the only way for you to realize your genuine career and life satisfaction.

On the other hand, if your talents and interests don't move you in the direction of being your own boss, owning a business could make you miserable. Why quit a job you don't enjoy, just to start a business that you won't like either? You could hate owning a business even worse.

In terms of your career, where are you right now? Career planning is a lifelong process. You don't want to make a change only for the sake of doing something different. When you make a career change it should be a part of your plan—it should move you toward your mission.

ᴖ Skills, Talents, And Values ᴗ

As a part of the exercises in Part One, you identified your talents and values. (If you skipped Part One, it is imperative that you go back and do the exercises before continuing with this chapter.) You understand that your talents are the foundation of your life, and based on what motivates you, you will be able to decide if you will be better served by working for someone else or by being your own boss. The type of work you enjoy and your life circumstances can move you in either direction.

⊰ Your Perfect Day ≻

Here is a fun exercise which can help fine-tune your vision of yourself. Write a paragraph describing your perfect day. Make it as long as you want, and be descriptive. You may use the space on page 229 or on the next blank, right-hand page in your notebook write, "My Perfect Day" at the top.

Before you begin writing, read the following questions. They might stimulate your thoughts:

- ❑ Would you eat breakfast?
- ❑ How would you get to work?
- ❑ How long of a commute would you have?
- ❑ What appointments would you have?
- ❑ What type of meetings would you participate in?
- ❑ Would you spend time on the telephone?
- ❑ What would you do for lunch?
- ❑ What leisure time activities would you participate in?
- ❑ What family activities would you participate in?
- ❑ What time would you go to bed?

Does your Perfect Day give you any clues to help you structure your life? It is amazing what you can learn about yourself by creative thinking.

⊰ Health And Emotions ≻

If you are not in good physical or mental health, you should think long and hard before starting your own business. Your personal life needs to be in balance—more so than ever before—when you are setting out on your own. You will probably have to deal with a lot of stress—can you handle it? What affect will these new pressures have on your family and other relationships?

How you work through your emotions is critical in predicting your ability to persevere. Remember how easily fear and anxiety can lead to self-doubt? You must be determined—and strong.

As an entrepreneur, if you're ill and not able to perform a task, more than likely it won't get done. As an employee, you could usually depend on your co-workers to fill in during your absence. This does not happen when you are the boss. Good physical and mental health is critical.

You have a thorough understanding of who you are, and what skills and personality you possess. Next, you should consider the characteristics which most successful entrepreneurs share. Analyze yourself to see how you compare.

Entrepreneurial Characteristics

All successful entrepreneurs are not the same. There isn't a perfect profile or a test that you can take to predict success at being your own boss. However, there are some indications that first born children, children with parents who ventured out on their own, and immigrants and their immediate offspring are more inclined to being entrepreneurs. So, even though there isn't a formula to guarantee success, there are definite characteristics which are shared by successful entrepreneurs.

At one end there are people who seem to naturally have everything it takes to run a profitable business with enthusiasm and confidence. At the opposite end of the spectrum are people, who for many varied reasons, are unable to run a business. And in between, are people who might or might not succeed, depending on their attitude and approach.

Since talents can be cross-transferred, skills can be learned, and beliefs can be changed, sometimes success at owning a business comes down to how willing a person is to change.

Most likely you have some characteristics which are favorable to being an entrepreneur, but you might need to acquire additional ones, or change some of your beliefs. Which is okay. The real question is: "Are you willing to put forth the required effort to succeed at your own business?"

After much observation over the years, I have identified nineteen *style* characteristics and nineteen *trait* characteristics which are evident in successful business owners. These two lists are not all-inclusive. However, the closer you come to matching these styles and traits, the greater are your odds for success at owning a business.

First, I'll briefly comment on each style and trait, and then they'll be listed again, so you can compare each one with your personality and mode of operation.

↵ Styles Of Entrepreneurs ↴

❑ **Calculated Risk Taker**

You search for ways to lessen risk, yet you are not looking only for security. You determine the risk-reward ratio, and then make a decision. You don't rely on luck. You've done your research.

Calculated risk taking involves some fear; it's a necessary response to change and growth. When you take a risk, you use fear to your advantage.

❑ **Hard Work/Long Hours**

Owning a business requires long, hard hours, especially at the beginning when you probably won't have the luxury of a large support staff. You will have to do many things you haven't done before, but you do them anyway. Seventy-five percent of the millionaires in this country are over fifty years of age, and they worked seven days a week to get there.

❑ **Action-oriented**

Although all of these characteristics are important, action is critical. Unless something is acted upon, it is an idea; nothing more. How many people do you know who have had "an idea"? It could have been a really good idea, but that is all it ever was.

Entrepreneurs are pro-active. They are self starters. They make things happen. They don't rely on luck or fate. They execute plans and get results; and they continuously learn from their actions and results. Taking action cures the fear of change and inspires self-confidence.

MY PERFECT DAY

_____

_____

_____

_____

_____

_____

_____

_____

_____

_____

_____

_____

_____

_____

_____

_____

_____

_____

_____

_____

_____

_____

_____

_____

_____

❑ **Decision Maker**

You can't wait for the perfect circumstance. Decisions must be made based on limited information. Remember, you change when it's necessary. Perfectionists will have a hard time with this. To allow the business to grow, you must constantly make decisions. A pattern of: idea, preparation, action, and success, without change is only temporarily productive. Sometimes you must move forward by making unplanned choices.

❑ **Accepts Advice**

You are open to new ideas. You request suggestions on how to improve, and you want to know about methods that have brought success to others. You ask questions, and you are a good listener. You are able to face the facts, even if you don't like them or agree with them.

You look for people who have already been where you are. They've already done it. You also consider attending classes on owning a business.

❑ **Eager to Learn**

Similar to accepting advice, you are willing to learn throughout your lifetime. You are open to change, and you want to know about it. You view change as opportunity, which allows you to make your business better. It's an ability to move beyond your comfort level; that's where real growth occurs.

❑ **Able to Accept Criticism**

Some criticism is warranted and some isn't. You can evaluate where it is coming from. If it is from a valid source, you will use the criticism to your advantage, rather than be defensive.

❑ **Problem Solver**

You don't view problems as obstacles, rather you enjoy solving them. Maybe someone has already found a solution. Don't insist on reinventing the wheel. Look to a training course, book, trade association, or franchise headquarters for answers.

❑ **Planner**

If action is the road to success, planning is the foundation of success. Don't structure a business based on guesses. Avoid rose-colored thinking. Get the facts. Talk to customers and competitors. Plan for success, not how to avoid failure. Set realistic goals based on "best knowledge available" projections.

❑ **Achievement Driven**

This is another critical characteristic. Successful entrepreneurs crave achievement. They enjoy establishing goals, and turning the goals into plans and projects. They feel satisfaction from making it all come to fruition. They're driven to accomplish.

❑ **Love What You Do**

To find true happiness and success, you must love your work. As your own boss, your business must become a part of you. Your life and your work become one; they support and nurture each other.

❑ **Detail-Oriented**

Entrepreneurs understand all aspects of their business. You need to know the details. You aren't bogged down by them, but you are aware of them because you are ultimately responsible.

❑ **Enjoy Being In Control**

Accomplished business owners usually don't enjoy being a passenger in a car; they want the driver's seat. They are uncomfortable when they aren't in control. When they are in control—they prosper.

❑ **Manage Your Emotions Well**

The responsibility involved in being your own boss brings with it many emotions. You need to manage stress, fear, enthusiasm, and aggression while using them to your advantage. Find your own personal formula which creates a balance in your life.

❑ **Enjoy Competing**

Most prosperous entrepreneurs view business as a competitive game—they love the action.

❑ **Have a Vision**

You are able to establish objectives. You have a plan and know how you'll implement it. You have a map and a destination. You have a vision, which you share with your employees, suppliers, and customers.

❑ **Manage Yourself**

When you manage a business, you also manage yourself. As the boss, you must motivate, schedule, guide, and analyze yourself. How you organize your business and your life is up to you. Profitable owners take the time to do it well.

❑ **Enjoy Reading**

There is a vast array of information you need to stay current on your business. Most of it is printed, which is why entrepreneurs tend to be readers. It is a part of their continuous process of improvement.

❑ **Willing to Make Sacrifices**

The long hours, financial commitment, stress, risks, decisions, criticisms, problems, and planning take a toll—both mentally and physically. The way you live your life will change. Your personal and business relationships will be affected. Be aware that the road is not always smooth. Plan for the sacrifices.

❧ Traits Of Entrepreneurs ❧

❑ **Confident**

Entrepreneurs are often described as self-confident adventurers. You must have an overwhelming belief in your ability to succeed—and you need the same level of confidence in your product or service. However, people who are arrogant or impulsive usually run into difficulty.

❑ **Independent**

Deep inside you know you can go it alone. You can prosper, despite a lack of staff and resources. You have a desire for personal freedom and you are willing to take the responsibility that goes along with it. At the same time, you know that your success is dependent on other people.

❑ **People Conscious**

The ability to establish rapport via clear and precise communication is imperative. Extraordinary interaction skills are a must. You must communicate with vendors, employees, customers, consultants, etc. A business owner builds up team involvement and works with others. You must be able to lead others by understanding what makes them tick.

❑ **Committed**

As a business owner, the business becomes an extension of yourself. You must be committed. If you don't have the time or energy to devote to the business, or you're not sure of the product or service you want to market—test the waters first. Maybe you should start a part-time business, until you're ready to commit to your life's work.

❑ **Flexible**

You must be able to determine where you should focus your time and energy. You see what needs your attention, and you give it, even if it is something you don't enjoy doing. You are flexible and do what's necessary.

❑ **Patient**

Be realistic in your expectations. Things rarely happen as quickly as you want. Stay with it. Reflect on the Chinese bamboo tree: during the first four years it doesn't grow, although you must water and fertilize it regularly. In the fifth year, it grows to eighty feet!

❑ **Curious**

You must continue to stretch yourself and ask questions. Curiosity keeps the drive to learn and improve alive. As an entrepreneur you deal with so many aspects of business that it is necessary to keep abreast of things.

❑ **Enthusiastic**

The more spirited you are about your venture, the easier it will be for people to join you. Enthusiasm is like jet fuel: when it fills your tank you will soar higher and higher. And since you depend on other people for your business success, you want them to know they can soar with you.

❑ **Energetic**

Your enthusiasm will produce energy, and you'll need lots of energy to do everything you want to accomplish. Also, the enjoyment of doing what you like will continuously create the energy you need for your life's work.

❑ **Healthy**

Eat properly, exercise, and control your emotions. Let your body be as healthy as it can be. As your own boss, you are the one who makes things happen. Your health is one of your most important commodities. With poor health, you won't be able to sustain your enthusiasm or energy.

❑ **Creative**

Most entrepreneurs are able to discover new ideas, unique ways to solve problems, and innovative methods of doing something better than it's been done before.

❑ **Responsible**

You must be responsible to your customers, your business, and yourself. You adhere to your promises and commitments. You take responsibility for your actions, and your employees'.

❑ **Determined/Persistent**

Most failures are attributed to the fact that someone just gave up. Persistence is a trait of success. To be an entrepreneur you must either have or develop this trait. Sure, it's usually easier to quit. But I can say with one hundred percent certainty, "If you quit, you won't succeed."

Stay with your goal. Keep taking actions and learn from the results. Be determined that you will get the results you are after. Overcome resistance. Don't let frustration bring you down. Sometimes the darkest hour is before the dawn.

❑ **Assertive**

The ability to make things happen is necessary. You must be action and results-oriented. (This is not *aggression*.)

❑ **Disciplined**

Accomplished business owners are disciplined; they manage themselves for the betterment of their business. When you are only accountable to yourself (you're the boss), it is tempting to go easy on yourself. Working only four days a week or sleeping in begins to look appealing. Don't fall for it.

❑ **Honest**

This is a critical trait. Prosperous businesses are built on a platform of honesty, integrity, and fairness. No shortcuts, no half-truths.

❑ **Sense of Pride**

You are proud of what you have done and are doing. You are self-confident in your abilities and your product or service. You know you are making a difference in the lives of others.

❑ **Forgiving**

Successful business owners know that the results they and others attain are not necessarily the results that were desired, and they are ready to forgive themselves and others. They know anger and frustration do not produce a solution. Forgiveness is progressive.

❑ **Thankful**

People who are successful are gracious—with their employees, customers, friends, and family. Life is living each moment with a gratitude for all that you have and are able to do.

There, you have them: the styles and traits that most successful entrepreneurs have in common. You can't expect to excel in all of these areas, but you can enhance the areas you are already strong in and you can improve in the areas in which you are weak.

Analyzing Your Characteristics

The next step is for you to examine the above characteristics and to compare them to your personality. How do you think you exemplify each style or trait? Next to each characteristic you feel you possess, explain how you feel your behavior exemplifies the style or trait. If you don't possess a characteristic, leave a blank space and move on to the next one. You can write your answers on pages 239 and 241 or at the top of the next blank, right-hand page in your notebook write, "Entrepreneurial Styles," and review the nineteen style characteristics. When you have finished those, on the next blank, right-hand page in your notebook write, "Entrepreneurial Traits," and review the nineteen trait characteristics.

Once you have completed this exercise, review your answers. Circle the characteristics that you believe are your strengths. With a highlighter, mark the characteristics that you need to work on. Remember, no one excels in all of these areas. But the more of these characteristics you can bring into your business and personal life, the greater are the odds you will prosper.

✨ Me Questions ✨

Review what you wrote down for the exercises in Part One. You identified your skills, you know which ones you enjoy using most, and you are aware of your career values. Now, answer the following questions. You can write your answers below or on the next blank, right-hand page in your notebook write, "Me Questions" and write your answers there.

Knowing what I now know, how strong is my interest in being my own boss? _____

Based on my talents, can I do it? _____

Do I need to develop new skills? _____

If I had to hire someone to run a business, would it be me? _____

_____

Is what I'm good at needed in my own business? _____

Can my values be met? _____

Do I want to take on new responsibilities, some of which are menial tasks? _____

Will I get to use the skills I enjoy using? _____

Am I ready for the stress? _____

Am I truly committed to make it work? _____

It is not important for you to be strong in all things. What is important is fitting whatever business you own to your talents, needs, values, and interests.

✧ Types of Businesses ✧

It is not my intent to guide you toward any particular type of business; however, I want to at least provide an overview of the three basic types of businesses you could own:

You could start **a new business**. This is the most difficult, though it could also be the most lucrative. Always review the risk-reward ratio. If you have a new idea or you've developed an improved product or service, you have no choice but to start anew.

Another reason to start a new business is if you could take advantage of *outsourcing*. It has become popular for larger corporations to spin off certain segments of their businesses, because it is more productive and less expensive for them to do so. If you have the skills and experience for this, you might consider outsourcing. However, if you contemplate leaving your employer to establish the same business you're now doing on the inside, be sure you can attract the right clients, so you don't promise more than you can deliver.

If you plan to **buy an existing business**, do your research. Why is it for sale? Will the customers stay with you or follow the previous owner? What is the business' reputation? Ask a thousand questions. Yes, there can be advantages, like: a recognizable name, a good reputation, a strong customer base, established vendors, and a positive cash flow. Just be sure you know all of the circumstances before you commit.

The third option is to **buy into a franchise**. (More than one-third of all U.S. retail sales come from a franchise, and over the next few years, this number is expected to rise to one-half.) If you purchase the right franchise, you should be able to avoid a lot of trial and error. After all, you are paying up front fees and continuing royalties for a proven system.

However, not all franchises are reliable. Research everything. Talk to current and former owners. Learn all you can about the franchise. Understand the purchase agreement and make sure it meets your values. Review your styles and traits. Are you cut out to own a franchise? You won't have complete control, and usually you'll have to make a large financial investment to start.

Decision Time

If, after reading the information in this chapter, you still have a strong desire to be your own boss, then let go of your past and focus on your mission. If owning a business is meant for you, it will be more than evident as you start the process. Some signs that owning a business is right for you are:

- ❑ You notice an increase in your productivity.
- ❑ Even though you're busier, your stress has decreased.
- ❑ You feel in more control of your life.
- ❑ You feel a deep sense of satisfaction, especially as you begin to help other people solve problems and improve their lives.
- ❑ You have more self-respect and you feel more self-confident as your business grows.
- ❑ You are proud of creating your new business and in living a new life.

When you do what comes naturally, *you* provide the security, fulfillment, and control you need to work happy and live healthy. When you are clear about your mission in life, and you take action to make it happen, you will feel genuine happiness and fulfillment. If you are right for entrepreneurship, that's what it will produce for you.

Entrepreneurial Style Characteristics

How you exemplify it:

1. Calculated Risk Taker _____

2. Hard Work/Long Hours_____

3. Action-oriented _____

4. Decision Maker _____

5. Accepts Advice _____

6. Eager to Learn _____

7. Able to Accept Criticism _____

8. Problem Solver _____

9. Planner_____

10. Achievement Driven _____

11. Love What You Do _____

12. Detail-Oriented _____

13. Enjoy Being In Control _____

14. Manage Your Emotions Well _____

15. Enjoy Competing _____

16. Have a Vision _____

17. Manage Yourself _____

18. Enjoy Reading _____

19. Willing to Make Sacrifices_____

Your next step is simple—but not easy. It's decision time. You must make a decision and a commitment to act. Here are the choices you have:

1. You can decide it's time to be your own boss. Great. Do it!

2. You can decide you're still not sure. You want more information. That's okay, but right now, figure out what you need to know and how you're going to do your research. Then, do it! Do not let information gathering turn into procrastination.

3. You can decide you want to be your own boss, but not right now. Before you start a business, you want to acquire additional experience and training. Okay, but you can still decide how you will get the experience and the training you need. When will you start your training? How will you know you've acquired it? While you're getting the training, can you begin other preparations for owning your business? Once you answer these questions, then you can set some goals and get started with your business.

4. You can decide you don't want to be a business owner. That's okay, too. You made a clear, sound choice. Nice going!

No matter what you decide, feel proud about making a decision. Few people take the time to analyze themselves and their position in life to take control of their destiny. Analyzing who you are and what you're meant to do for a career takes a lot of time and brain power—but the benefit will last the rest of your life. Revitalization is at your fingertips.

Your life will change the instant you make a decision. It's up to you. When you decide, "I'm going to do this because I want to better myself. I want to be more effective," then you've committed to improving your life. Your brain will accept this commitment, and your actions will follow what your brain tells you. The more you think about your decision, the more your actions will lead you towards your goal.

Entrepreneurial Trait Characteristics

How you exemplify it:

1. Confident _____

_____

2. Independent _____

_____

3. People Conscious _____

_____

4. Committed _____

_____

5. Flexible _____

_____

6. Patient _____

_____

7. Curious _____

_____

8. Enthusiastic _____

_____

9. Energetic _____

_____

10. Healthy _____

_____

11. Creative _____

_____

12. Responsible _____

_____

13. Determined/Persistent _____

_____

14. Assertive _____

_____

15. Disciplined _____

_____

16. Honest _____

_____

17. Sense of Pride _____

_____

18. Forgiving _____

_____

19. Thankful _____

_____

15

Escaping
The
Rat Race

Before reading this book, you might not have known why you were dissatisfied with your job or why you were unhappy with your life. Now you have a mission and a belief that you can accomplish your goal. You have specific techniques to use, so you can start getting results.

I've been asked many times if it is possible to lead a satisfying and happy life if you don't like your job. My answer is, no. Although some of your values might be met outside of work, and some of your most enjoyable talents might be used during your leisure time, you still spend far too many hours on the job to prevent work frustrations from affecting the quality of your life.

Think about it. Do most people you know have a work life that is separate from their personal life? They go to work because they *have to*, and they *live* their life during their leisure time.

Do you know anyone who seems to truly enjoy their work? Doesn't that person seem more enthusiastic and more content with their life? For people who enjoy their work, Mondays aren't different from Saturdays. They both represent days to live life—exuberantly.

If you've never experienced this exuberance before, then you are in for a treat when you do. Think about a time when you were genuinely excited about an upcoming event. Maybe it was a vacation, a concert, or a reunion. Do you remember the anticipation you felt whenever you thought about it? Did you daydream about it? How would you like to have those feelings everyday in your job? It is possible.

I'm sure you're anxious to do whatever it takes to bring this type of fulfillment into your daily life. Once you are clear about your mission in life and you take action to make it happen, you will feel genuine enjoyment and a deep feeling of satisfaction. I've said it before, but it is worth repeating:

Only *you* can fulfill *your* purpose. Only *you* can live your life. There is no need to be compared to anyone else. *You* are unique and have your own mission. You will find happiness through the use of your talents and skills, as long as you meet your values.

You won't find happiness in material things. As a matter of fact, I know a therapist who devotes her practice to very wealthy people. She helps them overcome their feelings of guilt, isolation, and low self-esteem. The biggest fear her clients share is that they will be at a social function and someone will ask them what they do for a living. In our society we are so defined by our work, by *what we do*, that these rich clients feel inferior!

My point: the further you remain from your niche in life, the more you will look to material things for meaning. However, you will quickly realize, as the therapist's clients did, that material possessions are not the answer. As soon as you know who you are, what you can do, what you want to do, and how you can make a difference, then you'll find what is best for you.

Picture a ladder. The first step is **knowledge** of who you are, which leads to the second step of **clarity**. The third step, **a specific career direction**, is produced by the clarity. A specific career direction will lead you to the fourth step, **meaningful work**, which brings you to the top step of the ladder: **a satisfying life-style**. With each step you take, your life becomes easier.

Like most things in life, there are two ways of assessing yourself and finding a job: through trial and error or following a proven plan. In other words, you can take action, get results, analyze the results, and modify your actions until you achieve the results you want. Or you can find someone who has already figured out a successful strategy and follow that process.

The guidelines in this book are proven strategies on self-assessment and finding a job. If you've completed the exercises in this book, you are well on your way to finding career success and life happiness.

You are at your best when you are moving in a direction. That's why this whole process of self-discovery and finding an opportunity can be so much fun. There is a great deal of satisfaction to be realized during the process. As a matter of fact, like anything you do in life, you will experience more rewards on the way to your goal then when you actually achieve it.

As you approach one goal, identify the next one. Always keep moving toward what you enjoy. That is what gives your life meaning. If you only focus on the result, you will surely miss the living of life. As a big poster in my office reads, "Success is a Journey, Not a Destination."

The more committed you are to doing what is right for you, the more your inner voice and your intuition will send you messages which clarify and validate your purpose. Have you ever said to yourself, "I knew it. I knew that would happen"? But you didn't believe in yourself enough to take action on what you thought. Your intuitions are based on your beliefs and experiences. They are guideposts. Use them to your benefit. If your intuition says you could get more pleasure from a different job or a new type of work, listen to it.

Acting on your intuition is critical at any stage of your career. Whether you are a recent graduate or in the middle of a career, you can save yourself years of frustration by knowing what you are meant to do and then taking the proper action to make it happen. Today is the day to make your commitment to change. Listen to your inner voice. Reach out for the opportunity which will revitalize your future and your life.

You *can* gain control of your life. Remember, before anything new can begin, something old must end. Life is forever changing. There is no valid reason for remaining stagnant in your career.

Earl Nightengale used to tell a true story of an African farmer who had heard of other farmers making millions by discovering diamond mines. The stories of wealth so intrigued the farmer that he sold his farm and set out to find his own diamond mine. He wound up spending the rest of his life searching, though he never found a diamond mine.

One day, as the man who bought his farm crossed a small creek on the property, he saw a flash of colored light amongst the rocks at the bottom of the creek. He picked up the glittering stone and soon realized it was one of the largest diamonds ever located. The creek was actually full of diamonds.

Yes, the man who sold his farm to find a diamond mine, had in fact, given up what turned out to be the most productive diamond mine in Africa.

The moral is obvious. You are your own diamond mine. If you take the time to explore yourself you will discover your unique treasure. When you make that effort, no one can stop you from being the best that you can be. But if you remain in a job that does not use your treasures (your unique talents and skills), and does not meet your values, you too, will have lost out on something of great worth. You will have sold yourself short.

Each day, think about how you will feel when you join the elite group of people who love their work. When your work becomes play, what differences do you envision in your life? How will it affect your production? How will it affect your home life? How will it affect your health?

I'm sure you can visualize positive changes in all aspects of your life. This vision of yourself, living and enjoying a new job or career, will help you persevere, overcome, and succeed.

At the beginning of this book I guaranteed that there was nothing that would bring you more happiness or joy than knowing what you were meant to do—and then doing it. I said you could get from where you are today to where you want to be tomorrow. Now, it is in your hands.

You can have a better job and a better life, if you want it. This is your project. Take control of your life and make your vision real. Discover who you really are—and all that you can do.

You have used your very valuable time to read my words and to complete several exercises that will guide you on your journey. Congratulations on making this investment in yourself and your future.

Now, as your journey continues, stay in touch. Let me know how you are progressing. Share any new ideas you might have which could help other people. But most of all, bring these words and exercises to life.

Go make it happen. You deserve it.

Appendix I

Research Resources

America's Fastest Growing Employers, Bob Adams, Inc.
America's Top 300 Jobs, Jist Works, Inc.
Career Guide to America's Top Industries, Jist Works, Inc.
Corporate Technology Directory
CorpTech Fast 5,000 Company Locator
Dictionary of Franchise Opportunities, U.S. Department of Commerce
Dictionary of Occupational Titles, U.S Department of Labor
Directory of Corporate Affiliations
Dun & Bradstreet Million Dollar Directory
Encyclopedia of Associations, Gale Research
Fitch Corporation Manuals
Hoover's Handbook of American Business
Hoover's Handbook of Emerging Companies
Moody's Manuals
National Business Telephone Directory, Gale Research
Occupational Outlook Handbook, U.S. Department of Labor
Standard & Poors Register of Corporations Directors and Executives
The Career Guide—Dun's Employment Opportunities Directory
The Complete Guide for Occupational Exploration, Jist Works, Inc.
Thomas Register of American Companies
U.S. Industrial Outlook, U.S. Department of Commerce

Appendix II

Career Planning / Job Search

Career Satisfaction & Success, Bernard Haldane
Change Your Job; Change Your Life, Ronald Krannich
Complete Job Search Handbook, Howard Figler
Discover What You're Best At, Barry & Linda Gale
Do What You Love, The Money Will Follow, Marsha Sinetar
Electronic Job Search Revolution, Kennedy & Morrow
Getting A Job After 50, Morgan
Getting To The Right Job, Steve Cohen and Paulo de Oliveira
Guerilla Tactics in the New Job Market, Tom Jackson
How to Get a Better Job in This Crazy World, Robert Half
Jobs: What They Are, Where They Are, What They Pay, Robert Snelling and
    Anne Snelling
Job Search 101, Brian Jud
Marketing Yourself: The Ultimate Job Seeker's Guide, Dorothy Leeds
Pie Method for Career Success, Daniel Porot
Stop Postponing The Rest of Your Life, Paul Stevens
Temp Track, Justice
Thank God It's Monday, Dr. Leonard H. Chusmir
The American Almanac of Jobs and Salaries, John W. Wright
The Complete Job Search Book, Richard Beatty
The National Job Hotline Directory, Marcia Williams and Sue Cubbage
The Princeton Review Guide to Your Career, Alan Bernstein and Nicholas
    Schaffzin
Very Quick Job Search, J. Michael Farr
Where Do I Go From Here With The Rest of My Life?, Crystal and Bolles
Wish Craft, Barbara Sher

Apppendix III

Entrepreneur Resources

101 Best Weekend Businesses, Dan Ramsey
199 Great Home Businesses, Tyler Hicks
Adams Streetwise Small Business Start Up, Bob Adams
Growing A Business, Paul Hawkens
Guerrilla Marketing For Home-Based Business, Jay Conrad Levinson
Guide to Self-Employment, David Lord
Joining The Entrepreneurial Elite, Olof Isachen
Successful Internet Business, David Elderbrock and Nitin Borwankar
The Entrepreneur's Complete Source Book, Alexander Hiam/Karen
  Olander
The Virtual Office Survival Handbook, Alice Bredin
There's No Business Like Your Business, Jack Nadel

Appendix IV

Select Internet Sites

America's Employers	http://www.americasemployers.com
America's Job Bank (U.S. Dept. of Labor)	http://www.ajb.dni.us
BSA Career Mart	http://www.careermart.com
Career City	http://www.careercity.com
Career Magazine	http://www.careermag.com
Career Mosaic	http://www.careermosaic.com
Career Path	http://www.careerpath.com
Career Site	http://www.careersite.com
Career Web	http://www.cweb.com
Commercial Sites Index	http://www.directory.net/
Communications Week	http://www.commweek.com
E-Span	http://www.espan.com/
	http://www.careercompanion.com/
Heart Career Connections	http://www.career.com
Helpwanted USA	http://www.iccweb.com
Hoovers Business Resources	http://www.hoovers.com
Job Center	http://www.jobcenter.com
Monster Board	http://www.monster.com
Nation Job Network	http://www.nationjob.com
National Business Empl. Weekly	http://www.nbew.com
Netshare, Inc.	http://www.netshare.com
On Line Career Center	http://www.occ.com
P.J. Scout	http://www.nationjob.com/pjs
Recourse Comm.	http://www.bestjobsusa.com
Resume-o-matic	http://www.ypn.com/jobs/resumes
The Riley Guide	http://www.jobtrak.com/jobguide
Thomas Register	http://www.thomasregister.com/

250

Bibliography

Bandler, Richard. *Time For A Change*. Cupertino, California: Metra Publications, 1993.

Harmon, Frederick. *The Executive Odyssey*. New York: John Wiley & Sons, 1989.

Moore, Thomas. *Care of the Soul*. New York: HarperCollins, 1992.

Nadler, Beverly. *Congratulations You Lost Your Job*. Charlotsville: MLM Publishing, 1992.

Pascarelia, Perry. *The New Achievers*. New York: The Free Press, 1984.

Peck, Scott M. *The Road Less Traveled*. New York: Simon & Schuster, 1978.

Porot, Daniel. *The Pie Method for Career Success*. Indianapolis: Jist Works, 1996.

Roof, Wade C. *A Generation of Seekers*. New York: HarperCollins, 1993.

Schwartz, David. *The Magic of Thinking Big*. New York: Prentice Hall, 1965.

Siegel, Bernie S. *How To Live Between Office Visits*. New York: HarperCollins, 1993.

Tice, Louis and Alan Steinberg. *A Better World A Better You*. Englewood Cliffs: Prentice Hall, 1989.

Index